EMPIRE GAMES

EMPIRE GAMES

The British Invention of Twentieth-Century Sport

ROGER HUTCHINSON

MAINSTREAM
PUBLISHING

EDINBURGH AND LONDON

First published in Great Britain in 1996 by
MAINSTREAM PUBLISHING COMPANY (EDINBURGH) LTD
7 Albany Street
Edinburgh EH1 3UG

ISBN 1 85158 842 6

A catalogue record for this book is available from the British Library

Typeset in Bembo
Printed and bound in Great Britain by Butler & Tanner Ltd

Contents

CHAPTER ONE

Soccer: The Irresistible Juggernaut

Association football (called Soccer for short) was invented in England, and has spread right round the world. It is doubtful whether there is any place where soccer of some sort is not played. English teams tour the Americas, much of Europe, and of course, all the Empire; the game is played in the icy wastes of the Arctic and (barefooted) in the tropics.

There is a good reason for this. Britons generally have always been great travellers and colonisers, and wherever their ships set out across the oceans they mostly carry a football or two. When the crews reach a port, all they have to do is find eleven local players, rig up two sets of goalposts on a pitch, appoint a referee, and within a short time, crew and locals are playing a match.

The Boy's Book of Sport, Carlton Wallace, 1951

On the last day but one of December 1889, a 21-year-old school-teacher from Birmingham disembarked, after a violent sea passage, at the remote Hebridean port of Lochboisdale and looked hesitantly about him at a rocky landscape swathed in mist and bathed with mild winter rain. Frederick Rea had arrived on the island of South Uist to take up a position as headmaster of the school at Garrynamonie.

The local political circumstances surrounding his appointment need not concern us much, although they were significant at the time. Frederick Rea was the first Englishman to be offered such a position in South Uist, and one of the first teachers who did not speak Gaelic. He was also, however, the first Roman Catholic since the Reformation to be given a headmastership in this intensely

Catholic island, and as such his commission was widely applauded in the neighbourhood.

Rea arrived in a district which, although part of the United Kingdom, was more alien to most of the people of England and lowland Scotland than many parts of Asia, Africa, Australia and America. Far more British civil servants spoke Urdu than the language of the Hebrides, Scottish Gaelic. Few, other than the occasional bagger of deer and gaffer of salmon, were acquainted with the customs – or even the whereabouts – of this lonely place. Rea himself, when the South Uist School Board wrote to ask for his references, had no idea where Lochboisdale was, although he vaguely remembered applying and supposed it to be somewhere in Scotland. When he was offered and accepted the job, his friends and relatives laughed at him.

'It is not easy to realise in these days of the aeroplane, motoring, and of the many facilities for comfortable travel,' he would write in 1927, 'how people of forty years back looked upon such a venture as I contemplated – less surprise would be created nowadays if a person proposed to take a school post in Spain or Greece.'

And less surprise, he might have added, would have been created back in 1889 if Frederick Rea had taken a post in Delhi, Melbourne, Nairobi or Newfoundland. By any useful measure Rea was transporting himself to one of the remoter unassimilated colonies. In the census of 1891 – which was taken in 1890, the first full year of Frederick Rea's residency there – the School Board district of South Uist contained 5,821 persons. Of those, no fewer than 3,430 spoke only Scottish Gaelic. A further 2,102 claimed themselves to be bilingual in Gaelic and English, which broadly meant that they had been taught some English at school, and just 289 were, like Rea, monoglot in English. The island's only link with the rest of Britain was a small steamer which wound weekly towards it from the port of Oban in Argyllshire. There was no mains electricity or water supply, no telegraph cable; the postal system was dependent on the ferry, and the telephone had not yet reached the Hebrides. There were no manufactories of any kind. The people survived on fishing and from the subsistence agriculture of their crofts.

Frederick Rea was met off the boat by the local priest and chairman of the School Board, Father Allan McDonald. They walked three miles from the pier to Father McDonald's dwelling, and Rea, searching for cottages, peered through the dusk past large, isolated heaps of turf and stones and earth, at an apparently uninhabited landscape. At last he burst out: 'But where are the houses?'

McDonald pointed at the blackened heaps. 'Those are the houses,' he said.

It was an alien land, an incomprehensible place, a district almost unrecognisable as part of Britain. Just as younger men were best suited to the administration of the more intractable dominions, so only a young Englishman could have adapted to the position of headmaster at Garrynamonie School in 1890. And because Frederick Rea was a young man and had a young man's interests, he would change for ever at least one large part of South Uist's venerable and tenacious insular culture.

At the end of the nineteenth century South Uist shared with the remainder of the Hebrides and the mainland Scottish Gàidhealtachd an antique repertoire of sports and recreations. The island's children and adults played a form of rounders which they knew as 'cluich an tighe' ('the house game'). They competed at a wonderful sport named 'speilean'. Variants of this distant ancestor of baseball were known elsewhere in Britain and in North America as bat and trap, or cat and bat, or one old cat, or two old cat, and most particularly in Lancashire and Yorkshire as trap and ball or knurr and spell (with which last word the Gaelic *speilean* shared a common root). The game of speilean in South Uist would start when a batsman laid a flat piece of wood (the 'cat') half over a hole in the ground. He then placed a small ball on the part of the strip of wood which was not hanging over the hole, and walloped the other half with his bat. The ball was thereby catapulted into the air, and if a fielder caught it the batsman was out. If he was not caught, he scored a point, and the nearest fielder to the ball bowled it at him. Once more, if his strike was caught the batsman was dismissed. If not, the first fielder to pick the ball up threw it at the original hole, and if it landed within a bat's length of the hole the batsman was out. If not, he scored again and took another strike . . .

The islanders played a form of pitch and toss which they knew as 'spidean', and a type of quoits called 'propataireachd'. Their version of skittles had been christened 'leagail sheaghdair' ('felling the soldier'). The game which children in the south of Britain enjoyed as 'king' was called in the Hebrides 'dheanadair' ('achiever', or 'trier'), and took the pattern of one elected tyrant whose function was to 'crown' new allies by laying his hand on their heads as they dashed past him towards the line which marked the safety zone.

They swung poles from the rafters of barns and tried to shake each other off the wooden horse on to the ground, and called it 'an lar mhaide', or 'the floor-stick'. The boys wrestled ('carachd') and rode ponies on the ribbon of white strand which runs for 20 miles and more down the Atlantic coast of South Uist; and they tested their strength at 'ciopan dochart' by sitting opposite each other with the soles of their feet braced flat against their rival's, holding with alternate hands a stout stick, with which one attempted to pull the other to his feet. The small girls played hunt-the-paper, and created intricate rhymes to accompany the many steps of 'iomart fhaochag', the whelk game, and led their smaller siblings through the rituals of 'MacCruslaig s'na mucan' – MacCruslaig and the pigs.

And for as long as the spoken and written records of their history could recall, back through all the busy centuries to the time just 500 years after Christ when the first few Gaelic-speaking Scots had tentatively set foot in these Pictish lands from Eire, they had played the team stick-and-ball game of shinty. They did not call it that: 'shinty' was a mainland anglification. They knew it by its ancient Irish name of 'camanachd', the bent-stick game, or more usually and colloquially as 'iomain', the driving game.

Two days after Frederick Rea stepped gingerly on to Lochboisdale pier for the first time, shinty was being played up and down the turf swards of South Uist, as it had been on every New Year's Day within and beyond memory. Large stones marked out goals on the broad and grassy machair lands of the west coast. A ball was made of wood, or of worsted yarn wound stiffly together, or of horsehair, or even of peat. Trees were at a premium in South Uist, and so the shinty sticks (camans) were often carved from tangles of dried seaweed, or crafted by folding tightly a strip of sail canvas. And then the game progressed, from dawn to winter dusk, with 50 or more on each side whooping and skirling up and down the unlegislated pitch, competing at a sport whose only rules were those established by tradition, whose only constitution was the goodwill of the participants, and whose only refereeing was the reluctant arbitration of men too old to play.

Within two decades of Frederick Rea's arrival in South Uist, shinty was no longer played there. One thousand four hundred years of deeply ingrained sporting tradition was wiped like chalk from the face of the island. It was not destroyed maliciously, nor even deliberately. Shinty was simply supplanted, like a thousand of its distant relatives from Buenos Aires to Smolensk, by a game which was almost as young and innocent as Frederick Rea himself; a game which was travelling like some benevolent virus across the shrinking world in the kitbags and carpet-bags and Gladstone bags of British soldiers, merchants, labourers, ministers of religion, and school-masters.

Frederick Rea was a keen sportsman. His personal predilection was for angling, a passion which was comfortably accommodated in the hundred fertile lochs of the southern Outer Hebrides. But he introduced his young charges at Garrynamonie School to many of the games of southern Britain.

He showed them cricket. One of his pupils, a woman named Kate MacPhee, remembered in later years how she and the other girls had watched jealously as the Uist boys were taught this fascinating sport, and then had practised on their own to the amusement of Mr Rea, who promptly arranged a match between the boys and girls – which the girls won, 'much to the chagrin and discomfiture of the boys . . . they drove us off the field in a shower of "pluic" [clods of earth] accompanied by shouts of "clann an diabholl" ["children of the devil"]. However, they were severely reprimanded by Mr Rea and were taught that such behaviour was "not cricket".'

Cricket did not catch on in South Uist. He introduced kite-flying, which delighted the children but alarmed an old woman who imagined that Rea was somehow hauling a large bird from the sky. He had a local joiner build parallel bars, which were installed on Wednesday evenings in the middle of the schoolroom floor, and he instructed the young men of the district, with a minimum of accidents, in a number of the new athletic disciplines.

Rea imported single-sticks and wickerwork headguards for fencing exercises, with dreadful consequences. He first demonstrated cuts and guards, and then asked two pairs to engage each other . . . 'after fencing quite skilfully in a seemingly friendly manner, each pair began to slash at each other in great fury: the guards they had been taught were ignored and they dealt each other tremendous blows indiscriminately on body, limbs and head and such was the force of their blows that, in a few moments, the tough wood sticks were reduced to splinters with little remaining in their hands but the hilts'.

After that the headmaster was reluctant to produce the boxing gloves which had arrived by the same post. He finally found a use for them when two of the bigger boys were discovered beating each other senseless with bare fists in a corner of the playground. Frederick Rea strapped the gloves on them and told them to set to once more. 'Little damage was done', and they retired exhausted, shaking hands and grinning, while their peers laughed aloud at the wonder of it all.

And then one day – we do not know exactly when, but it was a Christmas holiday between 1891 and 1893 – two of Rea's brothers appeared in South Uist. They were both sergeants in a line regiment stationed in the Tower of London, and they were both keen soccer players. The Midlands home of the Rea family had long been a crucible of association football. Three of their local clubs – Aston Villa, West Bromwich Albion and Wolverhampton Wanderers – had been formed back in the 1870s, and had been among the 12 founding members of the Football League when it was launched in 1888 by a Scottish official at Aston Villa named William MacGregor. All three of these clubs were dominant forces in England when the Rea brothers arrived in South Uist to visit their teacher, brother Frederick. West Brom and Wolves won the FA Cup in 1892 and 1893 before 25,000 and 45,000 fans respectively, and Villa were beaten finalists in 1892 and League champions in 1893–94. The fourth member of the Midlands quadripartite, Small Heath Football Club, won promotion as inaugural champions of the League's Division Two at the end of 1892–93. Small Heath would become Birmingham FC in 1905, and Birmingham City in 1945.

It is not surprising, then, that Rea's two soldier brothers took a football with them to Garrynamonie. They had not brought a pump, and so on the first fine day the three men sat in the schoolhouse sitting-room and took turns to apply their lips to the rubber valve and blow, until their lungs were aching and the leather panels were as tight as the skin on a timpano.

They then took the thing outside and introduced the game of soccer to South Uist. The three brothers booted the ball about for a while, smashing, to the schoolmaster's chagrin, a schoolhouse window; and then a neighbour appeared, and the most classically colonial sporting cameo was played out before the amused eyes of Frederick Rea. As Rea would record four decades later:

> We invited him to join us; but he had never seen a football before and was nervous. I kicked the ball towards him and told him to kick it back; he walked to it, looked at it, and stood and grinned again – I don't know if he thought it would hurt him if he kicked it, but he stood there looking most embarrassed while we stood laughing at him.
>
> I went to him and gently kicked the ball two or three times with my toe; then I put it by his feet and told him to do the same. Very gingerly he touched it with the toe of his heavy boot.

12

'Good,' said I, retreating a few steps. 'Send it to me'; which he did but very gently. After he had watched us three giving the ball some hefty kicks he gained courage and joined us, we played a two-a-side game, with Sandy most enthusiastic but observant of the rules about handling the ball.

Two more Uistmen joined in, and it was agreed that on the following day, a Saturday, they would all meet on the machair, those level turflands which were the traditional home of winter shinty matches. The three Reas made goalposts and carried them down on the appointed hour to find their friends waiting. The posts were erected, the pitch was paced out, the three-a-side teams were picked, and the game kicked off.

And then the occasion becomes, in the telling, suddenly reminiscent of the appearance before Lord Chelmsford's beleaguered troops of Cetewayo's overwhelming Zulu impis at Isandhlwana and Rorke's Drift. The six men had been playing for about five minutes when a number of figures loomed into view, marching towards them:

> . . . more and more appeared on the skyline coming from various directions, scores of them. Sandy had given the ball a mighty kick towards the opposite goal and dashed after the ball, when the foremost of the newcomers rushed forward and reached it first. He picked up the ball, ran with it, then kicked it in the air.
>
> My younger brother trapped it as it fell, and we hastily chose and arranged our two elevens from those of the newcomers. They seemed to understand Sandy's explanation of the game, and that no one was to handle the ball but the one in charge of the goal. The game restarted and all went well for a few minutes until the newcomer players became excited – then they would rush at the man who had the ball, catch hold of his coat and hold him, while another player of his side got the ball; the opposing men then rushed at this player and rolled him over while he lay clutching at the ball.
>
> By this time more men had arrived on the scene and, seething with excitement, they joined in the game. My brothers and I stood aside shaking with laughter, for there were now 50 a side at least: some were tearing about the field looking for the ball or rushing at each other, while in another part of the field a mass of men were rolling over each other, one of them wildly clutching the ball; if the ball came into sight again the excitement waxed

furious, and the whole hundred or so men would dash after it, throwing each other down, tearing at each other, all in a mad effort to get the ball.

Fortunately [concluded Frederick Rea with the satisfaction of a District Commissioner] the ball came towards me, and I put my foot on it, held up my hand, and called out: 'A mach!' ['Go!'] Perhaps hearing me pronouncing Gaelic sobered them, for they all stopped and I told them quietly that the game was over. Several helped with the goalposts, and we reached home thankful that no casualties had occurred.

News travelled fast on South Uist, Frederick Rea would have cause to reflect. The next Sabbath day the queues before St Peter's Church in nearby Daliburgh were resonant with the single word: 'fooot-baal'. The young priest there, Father George Rigg, called the brothers into his house, told them of his own fondness of soccer in his college years, and suggested a properly organised match – on New Year's Day.

Only one man seems properly to have identified the thoughtless impertinence of this usurpation by the professional classes of the island's traditional shinty fixture. Frederick Rea bumped into the retired Daliburgh schoolmaster George MacKay shortly before the Big Match, 'and he sniffed as much as to say, "What new-fangled idea is this?"'

Rea picked his side, putting the Eriskay priest and chairman of his governing School Board, Father Allan McDonald in goals, he and his brothers in the forward line, and seven quickly coached local boys in the other positions. Father Rigg's side more perfectly represented the administrative bourgeoisie, including as it did two other priests, a college student on vacation, two clerks from the estate factor's office and an accountant from the bank. Father George – aware of what had happened on Garrynamonie machair that previous Saturday when the Rea brothers appeared with their ball, and determined that the game of soccer should not again be played like shinty in South Uist – also obtained as referee a captain of the Cameron Highlanders who happened to be staying at the Lochboisdale Hotel.

There was a big crowd for the first proper game of competitive football in South Uist, and they 'remained outside the playing pitch'. Frederick Rea's side played to the whistle – 'which was a lesson in restraint to the many young fellows who had followed us from our end of the island' – and wound up winning 3–1. The Rea brothers from Birmingham knew about the science of this game of soccer in the early 1890s: '. . . if my brother on the left wing were tackled by several opponents, he swung the ball to me in the centre where I made ahead for goal, and, if pressed, I tapped the ball to my other brother on the right wing, thus combining our play; whereas the opposing side were individualists who, though good players and full of energy, wasted much effort'.

Only the old schoolmaster, George MacKay, was unenchanted. After the match 'he sighed as he wagged his sage head and said: "Ach, aye! But you and your brothers understand the game," and off he went without further word'.

George MacKay may not have lived to witness the complete destruction of shinty and speilean and cluiche an tighe in the southern Outer Hebrides, but he certainly saw the beginning of their end. They lasted not much longer. And the scenes portrayed above could have happened anywhere, and did happen almost everywhere.

They were imperial scenes. Not the most harmful or distressing of imperial scenes, perhaps. The implantation of organised sports may indeed be the only commonplace deed of Empire which was not only willingly embraced at the time by the indigenes of the dominions, but which is still welcomed today.

But they were imperial scenes nonetheless, repeated on a hundred Indian *maidans* and all across the high veldts of Victoria's possessions: from the local interpreter explaining the rules to his neighbours, to Frederick Rea's tickled frustration with the 'excitable' natives, to the fact that one of those footballing brother's bones would be left a few years later rotting in the sand at Omdurman; they were imperial scenes.

Soldiers and schoolteachers were the John the Baptists of the faith of association football and the hundred other recreational devices of the Victorian British; soldiers and schoolteachers and priests, and railway workers and miners and factory managers, took them across the world in a few short decades, and when they had finished their work the world would never be the same again. By the time that they had collected their company pensions and retired back to Hertfordshire, Rutland and Loch Lomond-side, around the earth men and women played and watched and understood identical games, and so a huge international network of sport became suddenly possible: a network which would quickly evolve into an entertainment industry so massive and so important that it created untold millionaires and broke as many hearts; bred corruption, riots, manslaughter, murder and even wars; felled governments, dominated lives, and enriched the existences of countless ordinary people. Faced so surprisingly with the ground-trembling roar of this irresistible juggernaut, the idiosyncratic, sweet old traditional games of the village sward mostly took heart attacks in its headlights and died unremembered deaths.

How and why did it all happen? What historical impulses were at work? C.L.R. James, the Trinidadian philosopher, historian and sportsman, considered that European civilisation's lust for organised sport merely went into abeyance between the fall of the Greco-Romans and the rise of the Victorian British. James wrote in 1963:

> A glance at the world showed that when the common people were not at work, one thing they wanted was organised sport and games. They wanted them greedily, passionately . . . Organised games had been part and parcel of the civilisation of Ancient Greece. With the decline of that civilisation they disappeared from Europe for some 1,500 years. People ran and jumped and kicked balls about and competed with one another; they went to see the knights jousting. But games and sports, organised as the Greeks had organised them, there were none. More curious still to the enquiring eye, after this long absence they seemed all to have returned within about a decade of each other, in frantic haste, as if there were only limited space and those who did not get in early would be permanently shut out.

The Greco-Romans, whose last Olympic Games were held in AD393, and the Victorian British, whose frantic rush to codify sports began in the middle of the nineteenth century, had at least one thing in common: an empire. Empires require discipline and impose standards. Frederick Rea would reflect of his introduction of soccer to the schoolchildren of South Uist that 'the fairness of its rules seemed to appeal to the boys who played both with zest and enjoyment but with due observance of a penalty for unfair play'.

Rea would hardly have regarded the game of shinty in this light. Shinty in South Uist in the 1890s would have appeared to him as more of a barbaric rout than a sport, possessing no civilised or civilising attributes at all. In fact, just 30 years separated the organisation of shinty and soccer. Before 1863, when the Football Association was established in London and universal rules were agreed upon, soccer matches throughout Britain routinely resembled that first riotous scrimmage on Garrynamonie machair far more than they resembled the exhibition game arranged a few days later by Father George Rigg.

But five years before Frederick Rea was born, soccer had become a disciplined, codified, responsible game: a game which Victorian schoolmasters could not only enjoy, but could also introduce to their flocks with a clear conscience, happy in the knowledge that by playing football the boys were learning teamwork, restraint, fairness and the meaning of rules. In 1893, possibly in the same year that his brothers arrived for their Christmas furlough carrying a football, shinty followed suit: the Camanachd Association was formed in Kingussie on the Scottish mainland. There was, as C.L.R. James suggested, only limited space, and shinty had got in just in time. The game would consequently survive and even prosper in Kingussie and other parts of the mainland . . . but not in South Uist. The rules and constitution of the Camanachd Association, the gentrification of shinty, came too late for South Uist.

A hundred years after those epochal soccer matches on the South Uist machair in the early 1890s, the visitor to that island who travelled with an eye open for sport would have seen effectively no facilities other than soccer pitches. Had that modern visitor stopped on the machair to watch a game, he or she would have been entertained by association football of a very high standard indeed, considering the small population of the place. The young men in the region of Garrynamonie School formed decades ago a football club called South End, which played in the Uist and Barra League. This league, which covered the sparsely inhabited islands of Berneray, North Uist, Benbecula, South Uist, Eriskay, Barra and Vatersay had nine or ten football teams. The combined population of these islands was, in the census of 1991, just over 7,000. The population of South Uist and neighbouring Eriskay, which had been almost 6,000 in Frederick Rea's time, was reduced to just 2,285. South Uist and Eriskay nonetheless fielded in the early 1990s no fewer than four senior football teams. The game which conquered the world had also conquered the southern isles of the Outer Hebrides.

In 1993, in unwitting celebration of what was possibly their centenary, the footballers of South End FC – men with the surnames of Frederick Rea's pupils and neighbours, MacPhees, MacIsaacs and MacDonalds; men who still spoke Gaelic, knew Gaelic songs and stories and traditions; but men whose fathers had long forgotten the games of the past – enjoyed their finest hour. As champions of their

17

local league they entered in a trans-Highland soccer cup competition whose first-round draw included the names of more than 100 clubs from across the north of Scotland. After a number of trips over hundreds of miles of land and sea, and a series of scintillating performances, South End reached the final, where they were beaten in a blaze of goals and glory. Frederick Rea and his brothers would have been astonished, and immensely proud.

'The Uist boys used to be,' wrote their compatriot Alexander Morrison in 1908, 'and in some places still are, very proficient at the game, the main qualities . . . being speed and dexterity.' The game that, in the 1900s, Morrison was already talking of in the past tense, was of course the game of iomain, or shinty. In 1993, hardly a single shinty stick had been used in competition in South Uist for the best part of a century. Sporting skills are easily transferable.

The pretty pageant which has been played out above was more than just a little local story. The sudden abdication of an indigenous sporting dynasty which had thrived for more than a millennium, and the triumph of the brash foreign pretender to its crown was no petty accident, and it was very far from being unique to the Hebrides. The essence of the tale of the Rea brothers and the island of South Uist is its universality. The dramas which were enjoyed on the machair lands between Daliburgh and Garrynamonie in the early 1890s present us with a stark and unambiguous metaphor of all of the sweeping contemporaneous events which, as C.L.R. James suggested, were, simply, so remarkable that it has taken us a century to bring them to terms. Having done so, we see that they were unprecedented in human history.

CHAPTER TWO

From Greek Games to Cotswold Olympics

It is almost impossible to tell just when, in the history of mankind, athletics started. Contests between runners and jumpers probably date from prehistoric times. But when we come to modern athletics – the kind we see on Sports Day and at the Olympics – we know that it was the Peloponnesians who started a series of contests which the Greeks of the north made into a great festival.

The Boy's Book of Sport, Carlton Wallace, 1951

In the beginning there were the games which evolved from the everyday activities of our ancestors. Fighting, running, hunting and swimming became (as a direct result of what some scholars dignify as the agonistic imperative of early man, but which was merely the bellicose contentiousness of boys being boys) boxing and wrestling, sprinting, archery and the throwing of discuses, javelins and hammers, and races through water.

And as humans trained animals and manufactured means of transport, so horses, camels, llamas, elephants, reindeer and even water-buffalo were raced; and oarsmen from Polynesia to the Great Lakes by way of the River Thames tested their strength and timing against each other; and methods were explored of making one sleigh faster than its neighbour, or the wheels of a carriage turn more quickly.

Those were the origins of sports. They constituted the recreation which reached their apotheosis in the thousand years of the ancient Olympic Games. How far back need we go, through our recorded time, to find their beginnings?

To the Sumerians who ruled over the scattered villages which lay between the Tigris and Euphrates valleys 3,500 years before Christ, whose surviving Mesopotamian art shows – in one instance – three Assyrian swimmers, two using floats and the other practising a useful crawl; who built statues of wrestlers unaccountably wearing hats and of boxers squaring up to each other; whose series of tablets known as the 'Kikkulis Text', which date from 1360BC, advise on the feeding and training of horses, and their preparation for races?

Or to the Egyptians, with their relief on a tomb of the twentieth dynasty (who reigned in about 1160BC) showing well-dressed spectators watching seven pairs of multiracial wrestlers and groups of stick-fighters; whose art depicted boys playing tug-of-war and tag, and jumping over distances and over high bars, and lifting heavy bags of sand, and chasing hoops; whose frescoes show us girls juggling, and swimming under water, and men rowing, and people whose efforts are obviously more playful than warlike, fighting with relatively harmless sticks from the bows of boats?

The Egyptians valued leisure time, and their children's tombs contained balls of packed straw bound in coloured leather, or balls of wood and of baked clay. The Egyptians had a concept of sporting excellence and demonstrated the fact by inscribing a relief of a bow-wielding monarch at Karnak with the words: 'His Majesty performed this act of athleticism in sight of all the land.'

And inevitably, by way of the bull-dancing Minoans, to the Ancient Greeks. According to Homer, the god Pelops staged a games meet around 1370BC, and 100 years later Achilles organised an athletics festival which featured chariot-racing, wrestling, running, archery, boxing, and the ritual sacrifice by barbecue of a small boy, who was then eaten.

When Homer's hero Odysseus was washed up after the Trojan Wars on the shore of the land of Phaeacia, he was able to leave us a fine account of such gatherings. After eating and drinking the Phaeacian king, noting with sympathy Odysseus's post-combat misery, proclaimed a diversion: 'Let us go outside now and try skills at various sports, so that when our guest has reached his home he can tell his friends that at boxing, wrestling, jumping and running there is no one who can beat us.'

A vast crowd followed them to the sporting arena:

> The first event was a race. They ran at full speed from the start, raising a cloud of dust from the track as they flew along. By far

the quickest was the excellent Clytoneus, who shot ahead, and when he reached the crowd at the post he had left the rest behind by as much as the width of a fallow field that mules can plough in a day.

Next came the painful sport of wrestling; and here it was Euryalus's turn to beat all the champions. Amphialus won the jump; at throwing the discus Elatreus was by far the best; and at boxing, Laodamus, Alcinous's handsome son.

Some Greek scholars have claimed that Phaeacia was Corfu in the eighth century BC; others that the place was Crete; and others that it was without the Hellenic diaspora altogether. It hardly seems to matter in the light of a sylvan scene which shines with something like familiarity down all the centuries. The Homeric Greeks may not have left behind any athletics records (the sundial being unreliable over matters of minutes, even had they considered such details to have been important). We may fairly assume that their sprinters were much slower than ours, as even in competition they put as much value on grace as on victory. Short-distance runners probably performed at a similar loping pace to today's 800- and 1,500-metre competitors; and even long-distance performers were far less effective. (The Greeks may have initiated the Marathon race, but they did so as an awed tribute to the first man known to have run 25 miles under stress – and it is noteworthy that even he, Pheidippides the practised courier, died at the finish of a distance which, two and a half millennia later, tens of thousands of ordinary Europeans were able to negotiate without much difficulty.)

But the Greeks, as Homer's description indicates, perceived sport as recreation and as therapy, not only for the participants but also for the 'vast crowd' which followed them to the track and field. Odysseus was invited to lose himself and his sadness in the thrill of the contest. Every twentieth century soccer fan will recognise that facility. In that, in their development of organised spectator sports, and in their recognition of such pursuits as physical art forms which were, like all good art, transporting and deserving of popular applause for their instinctive beauty as much as for their quasi-martial prowess, the people of Ancient Greece remain our creditors.

The Games at Olympia were themselves wonderfully documen-ted, surviving as they did for 1,277 years before the first properly literate western civilisations. We know as from our own childhoods the tale of King Iphitus of Elis, who called in 884BC for athletic competitions to be held at Olympia in his own Elisian Fields. For their duration a sacred truce would obtain. Nobody would arm himself in anger, or initiate any legal dispute, and no death penalties would be carried out (although a limited number of small boys still had reason to be nervous of the griddle). The terms of Iphitus's truce were recorded in five interwoven circles. The games would be quadrennial, and the four years between them became known in Greece as an Olympiad.

We know that in 776BC the 200-metre foot race at the Elisian Olympics was won by Coroebus of Elis: a popular victory among the home support. We know that by the end of the sixth century BC, when every Greek city-state was expected to have such facilities for athletics as gymnasia, athletes often worked through pre-Olympics training schedules for as much as ten months before the Elisian meeting. We know that all but pure-blooded Greeks were banned from competition, that prizes were freely offered and accepted, and that married women were prohibited from watching the events.

The format of the ancient Games would prove infectious. Day One was set aside for an opening celebration. After a swearing-in ceremony during which the referees plunged their hands into sacrificial blood, as referees will, they took a solemn oath of impartiality. Day Two saw the pentathlon and chariot-racing at which, as Richard Mandell has reported, 'We have eyewitness accounts of spectators abandoning themselves to frenzies of tension and advocacy. They shrieked, wept, embraced one another, insulted athletes in disfavour, and tossed flowers at those they adored.'

Day Three featured track events; Day Four wrestling and boxing; and on the fifth day a visitor to the Elisian Fields would have seen lines of men holding hands and dancing in rows; and muscular teenagers holding coronets of flowers giving thanks at the terrific altar of the Olympian Zeus, before leaping away with ribbons fluttering from their ankles and calves; and the visitor would have heard harps and flutes and drums, and the thrilling discords of polyphonic choruses; and he or she would have smelt, among the thyme and the bay and the sun-scorched earth, the oxen barbecuing on open fires across the busy plain. On the fifth day the visitor would have seen the last few celebratory hours of the one event which united all the disparate, contentious, quick-tempered men of the old Hellenic world. He or she is to be envied their glimpse of what the Greeks came to mythologise as the abode of the strong and the blessed after death, and what British nineteenth-century romantics, in search of a similarly heroic afterlife, would characterise as heaven itself – 'Souls of Poets dead and gone,' wrote John Keats in 1819, 'What Elysium have ye known . . . ?'

The thousand-year fame of the Elisian Fields spread throughout the civilised and into the developing ancient world. Alexander the Great took Hellenic sports with him into Egypt, Persia and India. A gymnasium was built in Jerusalem. As some locals were involved – and were encouraged to become involved – this was certainly early sporting imperialism. It lacked the po-faced spiritual fervour of the later and greatest sporting colonial adventure, perhaps. It is difficult, for instance, to imagine a Greek academician of the great era uttering the Hellenic equivalent to the whimsical lines of the late-Imperial rural English muse, Norman Gale:

> There will be a perfect planet
> Only when the Game shall enter
> Every country, teaching millions
> How to ask for Leg or Centre.

But when Jews of the second century BC were obliged to conceal their circumcisions in order to wrestle in a Greek gym in Palestine, some kind of athletic dominion was in operation.

And the culture pervaded Italy. The Etruscans took to running and jumping and boxing. The Romans, firstly as conquerors and secondly as tourists, swept through the Hellenic world and adopted the games. Their emperors Tiberius and Nero visited and competed in the Olympic Games, and Augustus started his own Actian Games in the north of Greece. If the Greeks had built the first athletics stadiums, which also accommodated horseracing, the Romans erected the first racecourses. Their hippodromes, built in most cities, created in the citizenry a clannish rivalry between the supporters of one set of chariot drivers or another – between the Blues, Reds, Golds and Greens – which would outlive Rome in later Byzantium, and which would survive most famously into the twentieth century AD in the Tuscan town of Siena (although its unmistakable modern echo is also to be heard from the *rossaneri* and *nerazzuri* of AC Milan and Internazionale on derby day in Milan).

But as the Romans grew in power and wealth, so they became coarse and brutalised. The Greeks may have been at home with slavery and sacrificial bloodshed, but the Romans came to relish the former and to wallow in the latter. When they came to combine the

23

two they hit upon a wonderful entertainment for a debased and jaded people: possibly the most perfect sport ever devised; but not one that could survive among a humanity which was, in the long, long run, bent on self-improvement.

Gladiatorial contests persisted for longer than we might care to imagine. It is arguable that certain chivalric areas of medieval warfare were little more than vague, disturbed and wrong-headed homages to the gladiators – certainly, no Roman captain in serious pursuit of victory in battle would have considered fighting it out, one to one, in ordered combat against a highly trained equal on a horse. As late as 1396 the Scottish King Robert III had built for £14 2s.11d an enclosure of wood and iron on a meadow by the River Tay outside the town of Perth. He ordered the Highland clans Chattan and Kay to pick 30 warriors each, and have them fight to the death inside this stadium to settle some dispute. A large crowd, including Robert and his court, watched the entertainment. (Clan Chattan won. Just one Kay survived: he climbed the wall and swam to safety across the Tay. The site of this latter-day Colosseum, which is still known as the North Inch, became the home of a famous shinty pitch – for no other reason, of course, than that it is flat.)

The gladiators had been finally retired in Christian Rome one thousand years earlier, in the fifth century AD. And a hundred years before that the Christian Emperor Theodosius had banned all pagan festivals, which inevitably included the Olympic Games on the Elisian Fields. The Games of AD393 were consequently the last. It was time. They were stained by corruption; disfigured beyond surgery by the grotesque spectacle of such as Nero prancing to inevitable victory in the chariot race. Afterwards the fantastic statue of Olympian Zeus was removed from the faded light of Elysium and carried to Byzantium, where like so many other irreplaceable artefacts of the ancient world it disappeared from the surface of the earth: atomised, it was claimed, in a fire.

But they cast the longest shadow, those Greco-Roman entertainments. They were destined never to be forgotten while men and women played competitive sport. They would be most revered 1,500 years after the last Olympics, when the most successful sporting imperialists sought the approval of antiquity for their own activities. But in the intervening years their shapes and forms and language cropped up, time and again, in the most surprising places, like a legion of the undead poking a hand occasionally through the earth that buried them, testing the air and gathering energy for the great revival.

In or around 1604 a young Warwickshire attorney named Captain Robert Dover first hosted on his Cotswolds estate near Evesham what would become an annual two-day sports meeting. It featured the games which – even then – were considered to be in danger of extinction in old England. Large crowds assembled to watch pitching the bar, throwing the hammer, shin-kicking, wrestling, jousting, and dancing to the shepherd's pipe. In 1636 some of Dover's poetic friends lauded the event in a collection of verse called 'Annalia Dubrensia'. They christened the gathering the Cotswold Olympicks, and the name stuck for 200 years, until the festival died in the second quarter of the nineteenth century – by which time other games were prospering, and an Olympic renewal which would sweep the world was just five decades away.

And early in 1728 a Frenchman visiting London was told that he must go to watch the gladiators fight. César de Saussure duly ankled along to Lincoln's Inn Field, where he discovered that: 'The gladiators' stage is round, the spectators sit in galleries, and the spectacle generally commences by a fight with wicker staves by a few rogues. They do not spare each other, but are very skilful in giving great whacks on the head. When blood oozes from one of the combatants, a few coins are thrown to the victor.'

De Saussure took his bench in the gallery, and was promptly hypnotised by 'an extraordinary combat'. A stout Irishwoman and a small Englishwoman took to the arena, scantily clothed in insubstantial bodices and short linen petticoats. Each of them announced their personal courage and strength loudly to the other, and to the gentlemen in the pit. Blue ribbons fluttered from the Irishwoman's head, waist and arms, and red ribbons from her opponent, in shoddy replica of the colours of the Mediterranean heroes of a past which they could hardly have imagined.

And they carried real weapons. Not the staves of the ancient Egyptians or of their own pitiful warm-up men, but two-handed swords more than a yard long, with a three-inch wide blade of which about six inches was honed, according to César de Saussure, to the sharpness of a razor.

The spectators, peers and commoners, placed their bets; the combat began; and after a while the Irishwoman 'received a great cut across her forehead', and the fight was adjourned while she was sewn up and had a plaster slapped on her temple, and the mob threw money at her opponent. The wounded woman was then handed a large glass of spirits, which she swallowed, and returned to the fray, only to be wounded once more. There was a second interval, during which she was revived and both women were issued with wicker shields.

> This third combat was fought for some time without result, but the poor Irishwoman was destined to be the loser, for she received a long and deep wound all across her neck and throat. The surgeon sewed it up, but she was too badly hurt to fight any more, and it was time, for the combatants were dripping with perspiration, and the Irishwoman also with blood. A few coins were thrown to her to console her, but the victor made a good day's work out of the combat. Fortunately it is very rarely one hears of women gladiators.

But not, by implication, of male gladiators in eighteenth-century London. There was little to slide between the contest witnessed by César de Saussure and any of the displays organised by the Emperor Augustus 1,700 years earlier. Death may have been more common in the Roman arena – although 'long and deep' wounds to the neck and throat in England in 1728 were as likely to prove fatal as not – but the purpose and the shape of the events were almost identical. They were spectator sport, only barely evolved from the everyday activities of our ancestors. Their atavistic grip was and would continue to be compelling. Paid performers would still be wounded and would still die in gladiatorial conflict three centuries after César de Saussure, and the victor would still make the best day's work out of the combat.

CHAPTER THREE

_____

Early Exports to North America

Have you ever played a game called Rounders? It is a game which used to be very popular in England at one time, and is very similar to the American national game of Baseball. Actually, Rounders was taken over to the United States by Englishmen, where it became played more and more. Now, just over one hundred years after it crossed the Atlantic, it is as popular in the United States as Cricket is in the British Empire.

The Boy's Book of Sport, Carlton Wallace, 1951

In the second half of the eighteenth century, just a few decades after César de Saussure's illuminating visit to Lincoln's Inn Field, two tableaux would have been witnessed in the colonies of Upper America.

On a meadow in Virginia, or Philadelphia, or New England, a group of colonial youngsters are playing a game with a ball and a bat. One of them throws the ball, which may be fashioned from tightly wound worsted, or from softwood, or may even be a conveniently shaped dried fungus, at the child with the bat, who strikes at it. Sometimes he or she hits and sometimes he or she misses. Sometimes the ball is hit a long way, and sometimes it falls dead to the ground. Being children, they know the rules which their predecessors on childhood's estate have already devised to contain these eventualities. They know them as well, and repeat them as faithfully, as the play-rhymes which they are also carrying intact from one century into another, rhymes which originated in the Great Fire of London, or the Black Death, or in pre-Roman British methods of counting.

They know, for instance, that the batter has only so many strikes at the ball before he or she must relinquish it or run from one base to the safety of another. They know that – in common with similar games – the farther the batter hits the ball, the more runs will be scored. And they know that if a strike is cleanly caught, the batter's innings is over.

An unfortunate mythology has clouded the actual history of baseball in America. In 1905 a wealthy enthusiast of the game named Albert Spalding, who owned a Chicago sports shop, established a commission of six 'experts' to trace baseball's progeny. This commission decided two years later that General Abner Doubleday of the United States Army had invented and codified the organised sport on a field at Cooperstown, New York, in 1839. Throughout much of the rest of the twentieth century, Doubleday would be uncritically lauded as the founder of this all-American pastime, and Cooperstown reverenced as its birthplace. In 1936 a National Baseball Hall of Fame was built there.

In fact, General Abner had not even been in Cooperstown in 1839, and his comprehensive diaries contained not one mention of the game. His sole qualification for this posthumous honour appears to have been that he was an old and close friend of A.G. Mills, the president of baseball's National League, who had advised Spalding's commission. If any one man deserved the applause of posterity, it seems – as later American sports historians have attempted to make clear – that he was Alexander J. Cartwright. Cartwright, a surveyor, prescribed the first 'diamond' with fixed distances between bases and drew up other playing rules for the first recorded competitive game of senior baseball. It took place on 19 June 1846 between Cartwright's club, the Knickerbockers Base Ball Club, and the New York Nine. The New York Nine won by 23–1. Alexander Cartwright umpired the match, which took place – and was this a beautiful accident or a wonderful design? – on the public land at Hoboken, New Jersey, which was known as the Elysian Fields.

Cartwright had codified the game, but he had no more invented it than had General Abner Doubleday. Clearly, baseball stemmed directly from the many variants of that old British game which was known as rounders, or as one old cat, or – in the South Uist which Frederick Rea discovered in 1890 – as speilean.

Perhaps most distressingly to American purists, many of whom had been prepared to accept an obscure and brutish foreign ancestry while claiming for their compatriots the vocabulary and finer points of the sport, this British game was also known back in its home

country as base ball. In the early eighteenth century a London publisher named John Newbery had decided to launch a series of
children's books. One of these, *A Pretty Little Pocket Book, Intended for
the Amusement of Little Mister Tommy and Pretty Miss Polly*, which was
published in England in 1744, contained illustrated pictures of different diversions. One of the illustrations was of the game of 'Base
Ball'. It showed three Georgian gentlemen standing on an English
meadow. They made up the three points of a triangle, and each of
them was adjacent to a small pillar, like a miniature standing stone . . .
a base marker. One held in his outstretched right hand a short stick,
the second was in the act of throwing, and the third – a fielder?
another batter at second base? – just stood there and watched, his left
arm resting casually upon a pillar. *A Pretty Little Pocket Book* contains,
therefore, not only the first illustrated guide to this sport, but also the
first mention in print of its – supposedly American – name. Pirate
editions of *A Pretty Little Pocket Book* were published in Worcester,
Massachusetts, and in several other American townships between
1762 and 1787.

North America was a colony of Britain, and so this game of
baseball was a colonial implantation. But it was an innocent, organic
process. Nobody planned it, nobody visited it upon the virgin
continent in order to improve the discipline, or morals, or spiritual
quality of the place. It just arrived, in the holdalls and the memories
of displaced Europeans. More than one American game would
originate in this manner.

In the winter of 1847 a battalion of the Royal Canadian Rifles, an
imperial unit which contained – not unusually – a good number of
Highland Scots, was stationed at Kingston in Canada, on the shore of
the St Lawrence river. They and their predecessors had been there
since 1783, lest the republican hordes should stream in from the
south. The republican hordes showed little sign of doing so, and
much of these British soldiers' time consequently weighed heavily on
their hands.

So in that winter of 1847 a group of about a hundred of them took
part in a recreation which may well have been customary since the
1780s. They strapped crude metal runners on to a wooden base
which they attached to the soles of their boots. They placed two sets
of boulders several hundred yards apart on the thick inshore ice of the
St Lawrence. They took up long sticks which were curved at the
striking end, divided into two teams of 50, and began to knock a
piece of solid rubber about on the flat, fast surface.

They were playing shinty on ice. That team game which Frederick Rea's soccer would displace from South Uist at the end of the nineteenth century, was taken to the New World by Scottish settlers and soldiers. Shinty on ice was not unknown in the middle of the harsher Scottish winters; in Upper America, where the mainland was routinely made impassable by snow for five months of the year, shinty on ice became a commonplace – and it developed into an international sport and a national obsession known as ice hockey.

A civilian named Horsey was watching those troops from the banks of the St Lawrence in 1847. 'Most of the soldier boys,' Horsey later observed in his diary, 'were quite at home on skates. They could cut the figure eight and other fancy figures, but shinny was their first delight. Groups would be placed at the Shoal Tower and Point Frederick, and fifty or more players on each side would be in the game.'

The regional bickering over which town or district of Canada was responsible for the 'invention' of ice hockey had grown so clamorous a hundred years later that in 1941 the Amateur Hockey Association of Canada appointed a committee to settle the argument. The committee found itself able to start work from just one shared position: 'that the rules of ice hockey had evolved from those used in a similar game known as 'shinny', 'shanty', 'hurling', or 'hurtling'.' Hurling is, of course, Scottish shinty's close Irish cousin. Eventually Horsey's diary, along with a lot of other subsidiary and circumstantial evidence, was accepted by the AHAC's committee as conclusive. They were able to find many other references to colonists playing shinny, shinty or hurling on the surface of frozen ponds, lakes and rivers, but none with an earlier dateline than Horsey's winter's afternoon in 1847. On that shaky basis they took the presumptuous but harmless decision to proclaim Kingston as the cradle of ice hockey, and to build there a Hockey Hall of Fame. (Which venture was either in faithful imitation of their baseballing colleagues south of the 49th Parallel, or to make sure that their neighbours could not pre-empt them with a museum of ice hockey in, say, Las Vegas . . . or, more likely, both.)

Whether or not Kingston witnessed the first time that an emigrant or a soldier took a shinty stick on to the ice of Upper America (and Kingston almost certainly did not), the position of ice hockey's British progenitor is secure. When the great debate which would lead to the AHAC's 1941 committee was raging throughout the 1930s, a gentleman named W.L. 'Chick' Murray threw his hat into the ring.

Murray, who would later be acknowledged as ice hockey's first legislator by Frank Mencke in that American sportswriter's definitive *All Sports Record Book*, claimed to have written down 'with very few changes, the rules which are used today' on 10 November 1879, while he was a student at Montreal's McGill University.

But Chick Murray did not call his newly codified sport 'ice hockey'. He called it – clumsily, perhaps, but with more regard for its true origin – 'shinny on your own side'. The name alone might have cost Murray his place in history (the AHAC's committee chose to ignore his claim). It derived, he would explain, from the fact that:

> As a small boy [in the 1860s] I played 'shinny' on the ice opposite the city of Montreal from November to early January. After that time the snows made it impossible to skate on the river.
>
> To play 'shinny' one had to have a good stick – no umbrella handle, or any stick that was cross-grained, would do. So, early in the Fall, the boys who contemplated playing later on, would go to the mountains and hunt for small maple trees which had roots which, when trimmed and dried, made ideal sticks with which to play the game.
>
> 'Shinny' at the time was a boys' game, the players ranging in age from eleven to sixteen years. There was one infallible rule in shinny – only one. It was never to hit the puck left-handed, the puck being a small block of wood, or a battered tin can, or any similar object that could be batted along the ice. If you did so, the rule was for the person nearest you, unless he was a close personal friend, to say 'shinny on your own side', and then to give you a sharp crack on the shins with his stick.

Murray seemed here to be understandably confused about the source of the name of the game (it comes not from the English 'shin', as many others have assumed, but from the Gaelic *sinteag* – pronounced 'sheen-tak' – which means to leap or take a short jump). But his depiction of the source of the game itself is clear, and it lives on. In Canada in the late twentieth century a rough, impromptu, knockabout game of ice hockey was still popularly called, not ice hockey, but shinny. 'Skate like a mad dog,' read the copy of a beer advertisement in the Canadian *Hockey News* in December 1988. 'Level everything that moves. Take wicked slapshots. Score the winner. Shower. Have a beer with your wingers. That's what playing a little shinny is all about . . .'

'If "shinny" is the parent game,' the magisterial Frank Mencke pointed out in 1948, 'then Kingston has no claim to originating either "shinny" or [ice] hockey, for the reason that "shinny" was played in Scotland many generations before Kingston was a trading post.'

Mencke was too fastidious. Scots – and indeed, many English and Welsh and Irish people – may have played for centuries what we would recognise as a crude early form of ice hockey whenever they took their shinty or hockey or bandy or hurling sticks on to frozen water. But they did not see it as such. They did not give the game order and shape and direction. They did not even dignify it with a name of its own – it was known to them only as an amusing bastard offspring of the preferred parent game, which was rooted firmly on dry land. The difference between originating a game and codifying it is great: many centuries may lie between the two. The second will not happen without the first: ice hockey does indeed owe its life to shinty. But without the second, without the legislation, centuries of riotous sporting life, hundreds of years of whispered history would prove worthless. The post-colonial twentieth century would kill the uncodified game stone dead. Only those which had been fortunate enough to attract an Alexander Cartwright or a Chick Murray would survive.

And when those sports of baseball and ice hockey returned to Britain, they came not as the spruced-up descendants of indigenous games, but as unqualified foreigners, as purely American visitors. As such, they attracted the interest only of a small minority. They had been too long abroad. They were unrecognisable. As early as 1874, just three years after the first professional baseball league had been formed in the USA, a group of American players toured England. The Philadelphia Athletics and the Bostons attracted a sizeable crowd to Lord's, but most were there to see 18 of them play an MCC 12 in a handicapped cricket match, and despite the fact that the cricket was interrupted for two hours so that the Americans could put on a display of what the English press persisted in calling 'base ball', the majority of the spectators left the ground talking only of the fine show the Americans had put up with a cricket bat (they scored 107 against the MCC's 105), and of the fact that the Philadelphia pitcher McBride had, when presented with a cricket ball, taken two wickets for eight runs in seven overs – while bowling underarm. The visitors returned home leaving hardly a trace of their own sport behind them.

In 1890 A.G. Spalding – that same Albert Spalding who would be indirectly responsible for establishing the myth of General Abner Doubleday and baseball's genesis at Cooperstown – offered financial help to any British soccer club which would sponsor a baseball club. Four football teams agreed. Derby County (which was still in 1890 no more than the soccer section of Derby County Cricket Club, and was therefore accustomed to a catholic mix of games), Stoke City, Preston North End and Aston Villa all took Spalding's cash and entered a league organised by the newborn Baseball Association of Great Britain. It lasted for one season, at the close of which Aston Villa were British baseball champions.

In 1933 Sir John Moores of Littlewoods Pools established a National Baseball Association. Amateur and professional leagues were set up in Lancashire, Yorkshire, London, Birmingham and South Wales. Between 1936 and 1939 they appeared to be almost successful, almost ready to stand on their own feet, almost capturing the British spectator, just as four decades later the North American Soccer League seemed for a tantalising season or two to be on the verge of altering American sporting tastes.

But as one failed, so did the other. Immediately after an English amateur baseball team had beaten its American counterpart in a five-match series (a result which the International Baseball Association rushed to acclaim as the first World Amateur Championships), the Second World War broke out. When the men returned to Britain, they returned to soccer and cricket. Baseball, the game which the British abandoned in their American colonies and left for their cousins to adopt, clothe and educate, would never be truly welcome back in the land of its birth. It would be regarded politely, with a distant respect, but never embraced as it must have been embraced by the likes of John Newbery and his children two hundred years earlier. In the failing years of the twentieth century British baseball teams were not even competing effectively in the 'A' stream of the European baseball championships.

Ice hockey – which nobody, not even a Highland Scot, would greet in the twentieth century as a long-lost son of shinty – enjoyed nonetheless a slightly warmer homecoming. Across the Atlantic, in the colony which had bred the game, ice hockey had already an imperial colouring. In 1893 the Canadian Governor-General Frederick Arthur Stanley, the 16th Earl of Derby, had concluded a five-year term of office in Ottawa, during which he had enthusiastically patronised shooting, cricket and yachting, by donating to the

Amateur Hockey Association of Canada a champions' trophy named the Stanley Cup.

The Stanley Cup, this unashamed relic of Empire – which was first won by Montreal Amateur Athletic Association, but very quickly became open to all – is the oldest trophy available to professional athletes in North America. It is also, according to the *Canadian Encyclopaedia*, the single reason why late twentieth-century Canadians remember the given name of the 16th Earl of Derby, but not that of any other Victorian governor-general.

So ice hockey came home, unlike baseball, with titled references. In 1895 two of Victoria's sons, the future kings Edward and George, were observed playing with bent sticks and pucks on a frozen lake in the grounds of Buckingham Palace. In 1903 a league of five teams was launched in Britain; and in 1908 a game was played in Glasgow (for the first time, they said, all unaware . . .). Great Britain won the European ice hockey championships in France in 1910; in 1914 the British Ice Hockey Association was founded; and in Germany in 1936 Britain became the first team to beat the amateurs of Canada and win the Olympic ice hockey title.

That was the high point, but the game did establish itself as a minority professional and amateur sport, with a small but faithful following. This was not, we may be sure, altogether because of a British preference for the games played with a bent stick and ball. The main reason for its modest success was undoubtedly that the islands which sent shinty, hurling and hockey out into the big wide world, had also a uniquely distinguished history of skating on ice.

The urge to order sport, to establish boundaries and acknowledge statistics, crept slowly upon the western world. The long centuries between the end of the Roman Empire and the beginning of the British one had not been a dark age of sport, as C.L.R. James erroneously suggests. They were rather a lengthy gestation.

Games were played by medieval Europeans, and particularly by the medieval British, which would become the transcendant imperial sports; and games were played by those people which would be drowned in time. We know something of these games, and we know little. We know that by the end of the first millennium AD a game was being played in the British Isles which would evolve smoothly into at least one sport, that of Scottish shinty, and consequently into ice hockey and a host of other adaptations. It was played with a yard-long stick, curved at the striking end, and a small ball. It appears to have been a favoured Celtic recreation, and as such it may well have travelled with those peripatetic peoples through Europe to their last resting point, on the windblown coasts of the Atlantic Ocean.

There is evidence of such a game on a carved panel at the base of a pedestal in an Athenian gymnasium of the fifth century BC. It shows five male figures with sticks around the object ball, and a sixth who may be an umpire. It has been said that the Greeks did not take easily to team games, and there is certainly little other reference to them in the Hellenic records, but no matter – the Celts in Britain played their bent-stick game between sides ranging from several hundred each, to just one against one. Three of those stick-carrying figures in Athens may just have been waiting their turn to challenge the winner of a head-to-head duel. Golf, of course, would come later . . .

The Celts developed this most seminal of sports. In Ireland and Cornwall it became known as 'hurling'. In Wales it was 'bando', which was anglicised as 'bandy'. In the springtime of 1777 a travelling Englishman named James Price asked a Welshman in the countryside of Glamorgan why the area was so denuded of ash and elm.

'Alas,' said he, 'do you observe those vast crowds of people before you drawing towards the sea?'

'Yes,' said I, 'I suppose there is a wreck on the coast.'

He informed me otherwise and said that they were going to a great bandy match to be played this day on a particular sand near the seashore where many thousands of people, men, women and children, will be assembled to see the sport; that it is the sixteenth match played this spring.

My companion further informed me that the inhabitants of a dozen or more parishes are in uproar and mind little beside these matches. 'Tis computed there are in each of these parishes up-wards of a hundred gamesters including young boys who are initiating, that each gamester furnisheth himself with three bandys.

If we add three more which are destroyed by unskillful bend-ing and the great number broke by thumping, thwacking and breaking each other's heads, not a bandy returning from some of these matches, it will make six hundred in every parish annually.

Bandy died in Wales before the Glamorganshire champaign could be entirely deforested. It achieved a minimum of legislation in the middle of the nineteenth century (when the teams were restricted to

20–30 players per side, the pitch designated as 200 yards long, and the goals as ten yards wide); but shortly afterwards it collapsed before the onslaught of rugby and association football. It left its name – and that of its curved stick – with us, however, in the term 'bandy-legged' (as shinty legated its own in the word 'shindig', and hurling in 'hurly-burly'); and when a form of 12-a-side ice hockey using large goals was developed in Scandinavia in the twentieth century, it was christened (and is still called) bandy.

In Irish and Scottish Gaelic, however, the stick was a caman and the game was called camanachd, both words deriving from the root *cam*, meaning 'bent'. Both hurling and shinty sticks are still referred to as camain; and the ruling body of the Scottish sport is the Camanachd Association.

It is the oldest team game which still exists in a recognisable form in the western world, and as such its influence has been enormous. The term 'camanachd' occurs throughout the medieval Celtic manuscripts. Saint Columba, who evangelised the north and west of Scotland from Ireland, is recorded as having played it. The *Book of Leinster*, which was composed in the twelfth century AD, tells of a game of camanachd between 27 warriors of two tribes at the end of the second millennium before Christ.

An illumination in Bede's *Life of St Cuthbert* – which records that the young Cuthbert was 'too fond of games' – depicts a boy swinging a caman. Cuthbert spent his childhood and youth on the Lauderdale hills, hard by the border with England, in the middle of the seventh century AD. Bede and his illuminators, who were patently familiar with this game, worked in Jarrow on Tyneside early in the eighth century AD. Celtic figures deploying bent sticks to hit a ball have been found on carvings in Norfolk and Kettering. In France its sister sport became popular in the middle ages as hocquet. Up until the end of the eighteenth century the game of cricket was played with a bat bent at the striking end: a bat which was only straightened out over the years, as this most emblematic of imperial sports achieved its own majority.

Such a game was not unique to Europe. In the islands of New Guinea an ancient equivalent survived into the twentieth century, which used a bent cane and a large, hard, round redwood seed. In Ethiopia to the present day a game called genna is played between teams of 11–14 participants, using a club shaped like a caman and a small wooden ball. There is little difference in the origins, or even in the form, of such sports – only in their influence, for the people of

New Guinea and Ethiopia were not destined to dictate the entire future of the recreations of the world.

When camanachd took to the ice in the winter of Upper America, it was marrying another of the oldest British diversions. Skating was necessarily a northern pursuit: it could hardly have featured on the plains of the Peloponnese – although the Romans, adaptable as ever, appear to have grasped the idea: deerbone runners were discovered attached to two of their sandal-shoes during Victorian excavations at London Wall.

Historians generally assume, however, that skating appeared as a widespread phenomenon in southern England along with the Norse tribes who subdued the area in AD450. Certainly, by the twelfth century it was a recreation. William FitzStephen, a confidante of Thomas à Becket, wrote a biography of the murdered archbishop in 1180 which was titled *Vita Sancti Thomae* and included an account of life in twelfth-century London. 'When the great fenne or moore (which watereth the walls of the citie on the North side) is frozen,' observed FitzStephen, 'many young men play on the yce . . .

'Some striding as wide as they may, doe slide swiftlie; some tye bones to their feete and under their heeles, and shoving themselves with a little picked staff do slide as swiftlie as a birde flyeth in the aire or an arrow out of a cross-bow.'

The diarists Samuel Pepys and John Evelyn each separately observed recreational skating involving the newly restored Duke of York (who had spent the decades of the republican Commonwealth honing such skills in Holland) in St James's Park, London, in the unusually bitter winter of 1662-63 ('with what swiftness they passe,' wrote Evelyn, 'how suddenly they stop in full carriere upon the ice . . .').

With such a pedigree, the next historical achievement of the diversion of skating is unsurprising – but not the less momentous for that. It became one of the first sports in the world to have a participants' club organised around it.

We do not know exactly when the Edinburgh Skating Club was founded. The *Encyclopaedia Britannica* of 1797 says that the club began 'some forty years ago', or in the 1750s. Another source offers 1744. If it was the earlier date, 1744, then the Edinburgh Skating Club was older than any constituted sporting organisation on earth other than Southampton Town Bowling Club, which seems to have laid down a green in about 1299, during the reign of Edward I; the Society of Kilwinning Archers, which claimed origination in 1483 and was certainly around by 1688; the bowmen of the Guild of the Fraternity of St George (1537); the Fraternity's descendant the Royal Company of Archers, which was formed in 1676; the Kilsyth Curling Club of 1716; and the Royal Cork Yacht Club, which was founded in 1720 – and if the Edinburgh Skating Club first met in 1744, it was exactly the same age as the Honourable Society of Edinburgh Golfers. There is no disgrace, as we shall see, in being younger than three archery clubs, a group of Scottish curlers and a coven of sailors. If it was not established until the 1750s, it was of an age with those other pioneers: the cricketers of Hambledon; the Jockey Club; and the Royal and Ancient Golf Club – and it certainly predated such an august institution as the Marylebone Cricket Club, which was not formed until 1787.

Either way, the Edinburgh Skating Club was an institution of considerable significance. It may have been, like most of its peers, an exclusive outfit with membership confined to landowners, lawyers (this was, remember, Edinburgh), the sons of titled men, and army officers (no women were admitted until 1910). But by its mere constitution it was flagging a new future for the sport as an organised, legislated activity, with certain agreed standards. Those early standards may have been occasionally bizarre – the Edinburgh Skating Club's entrance test insisted that applicants complete a full circle on each foot, followed by a jump over 'first one hat, then two, and then three, each on top of the other' – but standards they were, and the sport had not seen the like before. The Edinburgh Skating Club can now be seen as an early manifestation of the British passion for order which would transform the leisure activities of the world. The Edinburgh Skating Club's active life lasted for 200 years: it fell moribund after the outbreak of the Second World War in 1939, and was finally dissolved, apparently unaware of its own historical consequence, in 1966.

The Georgian British made further contributions to skating, and to organised sport. In 1772 one of the first sports books was published. Second Lieutenant Robert Jones's *A Treatise on Skating, Founded on Certain Principles Deduced from Many Years Experience* was ground-breaking partly because of the prescient detail of his coaching instructions, but mostly through the author's conviction that excellence in sporting disciplines was of greater value than might hitherto have been supposed. The Battle of Waterloo had not yet been joined, the playing fields of Eton were a muddy, unlauded patch of land, but Robert Jones insisted in his 1772 dedication that:

If any one should affect to despise the reputation of excelling in this amusement, I would wish them to consider, that merit is due to excellence of every kind; that the ancients paid the highest regard to strength and activity; the faculties of the mind generally improving those of the body. Could we trace all great men through every period of their lives, we should find in the early part of them, that they discovered in their juvenile exertions the sparks of those qualities for which they became eminent when called to more serious and important occupations. Caesar or Alexander, would have dreaded as much, when they were boys, to have been outdone in swimming, running or leaping etc, as they would afterwards in the loss of a battle.

A gracenote was sounded there, which would swell to a trumpet chorus one hundred years later.

(It is difficult to leave this sport in this period without paying one last tribute. In 1760 John Joseph Merlin invented the roller skate. Merlin, who had been born Jean Joseph at Huy in Belgium in 1735, was a musician and inventor who made his home in London. His roller skate was more advanced than he knew. Its wheels were not in pairs at the heel and toe, but in line one behind the other, like the late twentieth-century in-line skate, or rollerblade. Merlin toured the stately homes of southern England, demonstrating his invention by skating and playing the violin at the same time. Early in his career he took his instruments to a fashionable house in London's Soho Square, where he found himself gliding gracefully down a long corridor at the end of which – for he had not yet perfected the turn-and-stop – he shattered a huge wall mirror which his hostess claimed to be worth £500. Merlin was severely injured, and public interest in the art of roller skating dissolved. It would be revived a hundred years later, in the 1860s, too late for John Joseph Merlin to claim anything other than posthumous credit for his ingenuity.)

The two sports which British people combined in the overseas dominion of Canada to form the new game of ice hockey were, then, two of the most venerable of British recreations. They would also survive – suitably constituted and codified – into the twentieth century, and in that achievement they were lucky. Not many of their eighteenth-century fellows would see the close of Queen Victoria's reign.

By the time George III stepped onto the throne in 1760, Great Britain and Ireland were awash with a gallimaufry of the games of

man's devising. Most of them were played and watched by
commoners, and most of them were consequently deprived of status,
publicity and finance. But they were there. Gambling played a large
part in many of them, from cricket matches to César de Saussure's
female gladiators. 'Gambling,' says J.H. Plumb in *England in the
Eighteenth Century*, 'was an antidote favoured by all classes of society;
the wealthy favoured stocks and cards and lottery tickets; the poor,
crown and anchor, pitch and toss, or bull baiting and cock fighting.'

Plumb's was only part of the story. Like too many historians before
and since, he was blind to the huge role that sport, ordinary rough-
and-ready physical sport, played in the everyday life of the British
people. The ale-houses of the cities may have been interesting dens
of skittles, dutch-pins, bumble-puppy, draughts and dominoes; and –
in the days before urban sports stadiums – the metropolitan parks
might have offered nothing more elevated to the spectator than dog-
fighting and badger-baiting; but out in the countryside, where most
people still lived and, indeed, where most of the city-dwellers had
been born, physical games were their major recreation.

Not only bando, hurling, shinty, skating, golf and cricket leavened
the people's days. Football matches took place between village
communities, and even, in defiance of public disapproval and the law,
down the paved and cobbled streets of the towns – 'I spy the Furies
of the Football War,' noted one eighteenth-century lyricist:

> The Prentice quits his Shop, to join the Crew,
> Increasing Crouds the flying Game pursue.

At Leith in Scotland up to 20,000 people attended the annual
horseracing meet in the year 1790. At the Halshaw Wakes in Lancashire boys slithered up and down greasy poles and youngsters raced
on the backs of geese. Among the pit lads of North Shields, one of
them, William Fairbairn, remembered in 1803 that 'boxing was
considered a manly exercise and a favourite amusement, and I believe
I counted no less than seventeen battles which I reluctantly had to
fight before I was able to retain a position calculated to ensure
respect.'

For those whose age required more sedate exercise, there were
bowling greens, quoits pitches, and – in the north of England as well
as in Scotland – curling stones skimmed across frozen ponds. Each
Whit Monday in Brockworth near Gloucester there was the antique
cheese-chase, which had obscure origins in the establishment of the

villagers' grazing rights – a round cheese was rolled down a one-in-four hill, pursued by young men who chased it to a hedge at the foot of the slope. There was a score of different wrestling codes; and all of the athletics exercises which were enshrined in the annual curriculum of the Cotswold Olympicks.

There were handball, and stoolball, and battledore and shuttlecock, and that forebear of shove ha'penny known as skayles and keels. From the Hebrides to the Scilly Islands, there were all of those variants of base ball and cricket: bat and trap, where the underarm bowler aimed at a flap between two posts; cat and dog, in which two batsmen defended holes 13 yards apart, while the bowler attempted to beat them with a small piece of wood (the bats were dogs and the piece of wood the cat); the primitive creag, in which the wicket was a tree stump and the curved bat a 'cryc'; knurr and spell, which was specific to Yorkshire and Lancashire but was a close friend of that very speilean which Frederick Rea may have encountered in South Uist (the Gaelic *speilean* probably deriving from the English 'spell' in this case, rather than, as was more usual, the other way round), in which a small ball (the knurr) was triggered out from a trap (the spell), and then hopefully thumped by a player with a club.

There were marbles made of clay, or of glass, or even of marble, in which last case they were known as alley taws. Two London thoroughfares, Pall Mall and the Mall, were named after the game which was still popular in the eighteenth century, the French import 'paille maille'. It was played along alleys, sometimes half a mile long and preferably hemmed in by walls. Players carrying thick, curved sticks drove a boxwood ball a foot in diameter down the alley, and then through a number of iron arches in the fewest possible strokes. Nine men's morris was not a dance, but a complicated outdoor boardgame involving a series of squares drawn each inside the other, through which the players moved counters, or men, and manoeuvred so as to capture and remove the enemy. It spawned ninepenny morris, fivepenny morris, merils, marls, marrels, morals, morris, and miracles . . .

It was recorded that the inhabitants of Govan in Glasgow passed New Year's Day, as the eighteenth century turned into the 1800s, in throwing the cudgel for rewards of gingerbread cakes, and fighting with single-sticks with one hand tied behind their backs.

The actor Thomas Doggett put up the Doggett's Coat and Badge in 1715 to commemorate the first anniversary of 'King George I's happy accession to the throne of Great Britain'. Doggett, who preferred travelling on the Thames to using the streets of London, offered the prize of an orange-coloured livery and a badge representing liberty 'to be rowed for by six watermen that are out of their time [have completed their apprenticeships] within the year past. They are to row from London Bridge to Chelsea. It will be continued annually on the same day forever.' Thomas Doggett's wish is still being honoured at the end of the twentieth century. The event proved to be an enormously popular entertainment. 'Dempster and I,' James Boswell told his journal on 1 August 1763, 'went upon the Thames and saw the watermen row for Doggett's Badge and other prizes. We saw most excellent sport.'

In Cymru, as Jan Morris records in *The Matter of Wales*, the sport of 'cnapan' was really more a battle than a game, and it was played stark naked.

> In open country without goals or limits, anything up to 1,500 men fought to get the 'cnapan', a slippery bowl of heavy wood, into the territory of one village or the other. The play swung back and forth, over hedge, ditch and meadow, all those hundreds of nude figures racing across the churned-up fields, hurling the cnapan here and there, kicking, hitting and wrestling one another, sometimes urged along by horsemen, and forcibly bringing into the action anyone who happened to be near. At least according to one seventeenth-century observer, the game was played in good humour, and the players went home after the match, bleeding and bruised, 'laughing and merrily jesting at their harmes, telling their adversaries how he brake his head, to another that he strocke him on the face, and how he repayed the same to him again, and all this in good myrth, without grudge or hatred'.

Some historians claim that between the withdrawal of the Romans and the accession of Queen Victoria, popular sport in Britain was limited to jousting, archery, bull-baiting, illegal football and hurling, and the recreations that one invariably discovers to be listed under 'sport' in the indexes of travel guides published before 1960 – hunting, shooting and fishing. Most of the myriad remainder has been ignored, chiefly because their participants and most of their spectators did not write the histories or the travel guides; and partly because of the lazy assumption that rowdy games were all but eliminated by either the famous Stuart decrees against non-martial leisure pursuits, or – if they survived those prohibitions – by the Puritan revolution. The latter was not set as firmly against sport as we have chosen to believe. James Melville, who attended the village school of Logie-Montrose during the Scottish Reformation in the sixteenth century, assures us that as well as the catechism, prayers and scripture, Latin and French, Horace, Virgil and Erasmus, he was taught archery, fencing, swimming, wrestling, running, jumping and golf.

The games were ever there, in a ferment of inventive recreational behaviour which was certainly unique within the continent of Europe, and was probably globally peculiar to Great Britain, with its improved wealth and leisure time, its young imperial curiosity, and the sense of comparative personal liberty which was the pretension, if not the aspiration, of many of its citizens. And those games which were hidden from the reading classes, rather than the jousts and the grouse moor, would be the ones with staying power: they, and not the sport of their superiors, would be the foundation stones of the new world order.

(Jousting on horseback had in fact died out in Tudor times, to be replaced by the dismounted combats which evolved into fencing, and by small boys riding hobby horses. Tilting at the quintain survived for longer – the quintain being an inanimate wooden target which, if struck inaccurately by a mounted or a rambling foe, swung round and smote the tilter. A properly historical joust was witnessed in 1969 in a meadow in southern England, but its participants were stuntmen who had learned their trade in filmed recreations of *Merrie England*.)

Into this busy arena marched the pedestrians: the pioneers of time-trials, the heralds of the record books. As much as to the clubs and their codes and constitutions, as much as to the inventors of equipment and the authors of coaching manuals and the eager young men scribbling down a rough set of rules, the world of sport would owe a large debt to these distant avant-couriers. There were many of them, and they came in most shapes and sizes, of every age and ambition, from all the airts of the United Kingdom.

On a Friday morning early in October 1790, an old man left the village of Brentford to walk along the Great Western Road into the city of London. He made a slow start. His eyes were rheumy, dim and languid, and at the age of 102 years he stood just five feet five inches tall – two inches shorter than the maximum height of his prime. His joints and centenarian muscles at first were stiff, but as he found a familiar marching stride the old man fell into an easy, almost jaunty motion, and he turned at the first milestone to look back with an air of triumph at the thin scattering of spectators who were lining his way.

He had two hours and a half to cover the ten miles between Brentford and Hyde Park Corner, if he was to collect a wager of 100 guineas, a wager upon which the future comfort of his 48-year-old wife and their nine-year-old son depended. After seven miles, which were accomplished at the rate of a mile every 15 minutes, the old man reached the outlying township of Kensington, a farming community which was being slowly dragged into the suburban maw of the metropolis. Here the crowds were thicker and he noticed bets being placed at the side of the road. Mischievously, he pretended to fail in his stride. He stumbled slightly, and his legs seemed to lose their strength. A flurry of wagers and promissory notes changed hands and the spectators chattered their concern.

The odds having lengthened and the new bets placed, and the fields that would become Kensington Gardens having appeared in sight, the old man cheerfully abandoned his charade and picked up his pace again. The thickening crowd applauded. Turning to them, he cried out: 'Now, my lads, I'll show you some sport!'

A large number of people had gathered at Knightsbridge, a mile from Hyde Park Corner. Men spilled on to the street and children ran about his path. His passage was briefly obstructed, but he forced a route through the throng and lengthened his stride along Kensington Gore. At the junction between Constitution Hill and Park Lane, at the south-east corner of Hyde Park, he stopped walking. Loud huzzas filled the air. The timekeeper announced that he had completed the distance in two hours, twenty-two and a half minutes.

His lined face cracked into a grin and he pocketed 100 guineas. He emerged briefly from a cluster of backslappers to announce that, if there were any takers, he would walk from London to York at the same speed, for as many guineas as there were milestones on the road . . .

His name was Donald MacLeod. He was an old soldier who had been refused a King's List pension of one shilling a day, and in order to support himself and his family he had turned to what could be described as professional athletics. Donald MacLeod was, in the expression of his time, a 'pedestrian'. He set his legs against the clock, under the sponsorship of some society beau who would plan to recoup his capital through betting, or who might just be doing it for the reflected light and for the hell of the thing. Brentford to Hyde Park Corner would be the last sponsored walk of this little-known competitor. He never did walk from London to York: he died in the following year, 1791, at the age of 103.

By the end of the eighteenth century, expensive stopwatches could accurately measure time to within one-fifth of a second, and ordinary timepieces were reliable to the half-minute. A fresh dimension of sporting interest was thereby made available to the Georgian British, which had not been allowed to the Greeks or the Romans. They could compete not only against each other, but also against time – and against other people's times which may have been registered far away and in another season.

The pedestrians were the first to exploit this new facility, and the growing public interest in statistics and records. They were the first professional field athletes of the modern world. Their calling probably originated in the requirements of the aristocracy for seeking out the fleetest footmen. These footmen, who routinely ran alongside the coaches and teams of horses, were in considerable demand for the most practical reasons. Lady Berkeley of Beverston Castle once sent her Irish footman Langham on a round trip of 148 miles to fetch some medicine. Langham completed the distance in 42 hours, including time spent in taking a short nap. Such men as Langham, reasoned their employers, must be worth betting on, and it was but a short step from that conclusion to pitting Langham against Langham over ten, 50, or 100 miles while the dukes and duchesses lodged the 500 guinea stakes and cheered them on.

Pedestrianism was not entirely a proletarian pursuit. Robert Carey, who would become the first Earl of Monmouth – and who is best remembered for riding between London and Edinburgh in three days in 1603, to deliver to James VI of Scotland the news that Elizabeth of England was dead and the way was consequently open for this Stuart to become James I of England as well as VI of Scotland – had in 1589 walked from England to Portugal in just 12 days to keep the company of Robert Devereux, the Earl of Essex. (The feat so impressed Essex, as it was doubtless intended to do, that he gave Carey £2,000, which four hundred years later would have been worth one million. The Earl of Essex was, at the time, £20,000 in debt.)

And one of the most celebrated of the Georgian pedestrians was a putative Scottish aristocrat. Robert Barclay Allardice was a putative aristocrat only because he made unsuccessful claims on the earldoms of Airth, Strathern, and Monteith before dying a commoner. But

45

'Captain Barclay' was a king among walkers. In 1801, at the age of 22, he walked round and round a muddy park until he had completed an estimated 110 miles in 19 hours and 27 minutes. In the June and July of 1809 he accomplished the feat which would gain him unusual recognition in the *Dictionary of National Biography*: down at London's Haymarket he walked one mile in each of 1,000 successive hours; losing 32 pounds in the process.

These activities, which would seem vaguely puzzling to the supporters of later, more highly evolved athletics events, were widespread. In 1816 a former smuggler known as Baker walked around a public common near Rochester for 21 days, covering an estimated 1,010 miles. In 1817 he set out to double his record, and walked in circles on Wormwood Scrubs for 42 days, until he had completed 2,000 miles.

They spread, inevitably, to the dominions. Early pedestrian races in nineteenth-century Australia attracted large crowds, and the entrants were frequently handicapped by having to carry certain burdens, such as a jockey. One of the most celebrated Australian pedestrians was William Francis King, also known as 'The Flying Pieman', who walked in the 1840s from Campbelltown to Sydney in eight hours, and from Sydney to Parramatta in under seven hours, handicapped all the way by the presence, slung across his shoulders as weights, of dead animals.

The 'peds' were professionals. They operated in the centuries before anybody chose to elevate sporting activity into a quasi-mystical ethic, and they did what they did – if not entirely or always for the money – usually with a wager-stake or a sponsor's purse in mind. And as professionals, they followed the money: to Australia, where Ireland's Tom Malone and Frank 'Scurry' Hewitt and the English Harry Hutchins and Albert Bird travelled in the nineteenth century; and across the Atlantic to the United States of America. The American sports historian Ted Vincent told the story of a young American Indian named R.F. Leonard, who was – like Donald MacLeod – an impoverished former soldier, and who set out in 1869 to walk 100 miles in 24 hours . . .

> He had no previous competitions in distance walking, but now he was trying to make himself $20 by a pedestrian feat, to be accomplished by covering some two hundred times a course through the streets of St Joseph, Missouri. He began at midnight, the usual starting time for distance-walking tests. It was pouring

rain and he had to carry a lantern to see his way. By early morning a sizable crowd had gathered to cheer Leonard on, and some among them offered extra pay if he covered the hundred miles before midnight.

Others began wagering with one another on the prospect. By noon he had walked 56 miles. Around two in the afternoon he asked for a whip, with which he slapped his legs as he went. By dark a man was following behind Leonard providing the stimulation of the whip. A man on either side of him kept pace and watched to catch him if he fell. Leonard went through the last miles in fits and starts, and in much agony, completing the 100 miles 21 minutes ahead of time. He was hoisted from the ground and carried aloft by the crowd, but . . . he knew little of the celebration, having passed out in exhaustion.

Leonard may have walked for just $20, but irresistible rewards were occasionally offered by the Americans. The heir to a steamboat fortune John Cox Stevens offered in 1835 $1,000 to any man who could run ten miles in less than an hour. Enormous crowds of up to 50,000 people began to assemble at racecourses to see human beings compete on the tracks. In 1844 30,000 spectators gathered at the Beacon Raceway near Hoboken, New Jersey to watch an 'England versus America' ten-mile challenge for a winner's purse of $1,000. The favourite was a renowned English 'ped' named John Barlow. He finished in third place behind a compatriot and the winner, a New York chair gilder called John Gildersleeve.

It was the first stage of a sting. Barlow asked for a re-match, which was naturally granted. A couple of months later the New Jersey crowd had risen to 40,000 ('an army three times larger than that with which Napoleon made his Italian campaign,' commented the magazine Spirit of the Times), the winner's stake to $1,400, and the betting odds were more generous to the English peds. Gildersleeve actually ran a faster race than earlier in the year, but he finished in fourth place behind two Englishmen – one of whom, the winner John Barlow, led from start to finish and established a new ten-mile record of 54 minutes 21 seconds. Only later was it discovered by suspicious Americans that Barlow had, back in the old country, a record of disqualification for fixing races.

But no matter. As surely as those colonial children had introduced base ball to America, and those imperial troops had taken ice hockey to Canada, so John Barlow and his fellows had carried the competitive pedestrianism of Donald MacLeod and Captain Barclay to the United States. They would not be the last to export sport, but they did it innocently, for the joy of the game (and in Barlow's case a healthy love of the money). They were following no great scheme: that would come later. The games which they left behind had few fixed codes and consequently invited adoption and amendment by independent souls such as the Americans. Nonetheless their legacy – however unintentionally it may have been bequeathed – was a large one.

CHAPTER FOUR

Clubs, Codes and Constitutions

There was a time when Archery was so essential to the defence of England that a king (Edward III) issued a proclamation forbidding football because it interfered with archery practice. That was in 1349. He must have been a very far-seeing king, because some 66 years later there was fought that great battle which has been regarded ever since as a triumph of archery tactics in war – Agincourt.

Archery is no longer needed as a defence in war; nevertheless it still has a great following and is a most popular sport in many parts of the world, particularly in Great Britain.

The Boy's Book of Sport, Carlton Wallace, 1951

The Georgian British – into which category, for the purposes of this story, we might carelessly throw all of those who ran, swam, skated, and played with a ball between 1700 and around 1850 – were not particularly bothered whether or not foreigners played their games. Indeed, they considered foreigners by and large to be incapable of doing so (an attitude which would survive well into the twentieth century, with painful consequences).

'On Monday last,' read a report in the London *Times* on 2 May 1786, 'a cricket match was played by some English gentlemen, in the Champs Elysées. His Grace of Dorset was, as usual, the most distinguished for skill and activity. The French, however, cannot imitate us in such vigorous exertions of the body; so that we seldom see them enter the lists.'

Few men can have tried harder than John Frederick Sackville, the third Duke of Dorset, to introduce cricket to the Parisians during his tenure in their city as ambassador-extraordinary to France from 1783 until the disconcerting revolution of 1789 necessitated his speedy departure for Dover – where he arrived just in time to turn around the Surrey Cricket Club, which was on its heedless way to Paris at his invitation on a short evangelical tour. Before 1789 he set up wickets on the Champs Elysées (the French Elisian Fields, of course) at every available opportunity. But he failed to convert the Gallic soul, and the English did not much mind that he had failed. It gave them the opportunity to recount a compendium of wonderfully self-serving stories.

As an author calling himself the 'Sportsman in France' would relate:

> We got up a tolerably good match behind the Hotel Royal, on the beach at Dieppe, for the amusement of the Duchess de Berri, in the year 1829.
>
> We mustered, with some difficulty, two elevens; the bowlers pitched their balls with scientific precision; the batters defended their wickets with great skill; short and long stops were on the alert; in fact, all the performers acquitted themselves most admirably.
>
> As soon as the first innings were over, one of the party who had been most active in the display of his athletic powers, approached the Duchess's carriage in the expectation of being complimented on his exertions; instead of which, one of the suite asked the gentleman, to his utter dismay and confusion, when this game of 'creekay' was going to begin!

And so it would prove throughout Europe: they wilfully refused to understand. When the Paris Cricket Club played Sir Robert Clifton's Eleven from Nottingham in France in the May of 1864, all but one of the Parisians were Englishmen (and they still got thrashed by an innings and 124 runs). Three months later the PCC travelled to Hamburg to play in a 'France versus Germany' international. This time the Paris Eleven won, by an innings and 41 runs, against a 'German' team made up of expatriate Englishmen from Frankfurt and British tourists in Hamburg. If the locals refused to defend their own national sporting honour – why then, willing Englishmen would do it for them! There were, to be sure, German spectators, who 'watched the proceedings with a marked attention, due probably rather to curiosity than to a critical admiration, for it was discovered to be the more generally received opinion that the game was to be played upon horses, which, up to the conclusion of the day's sport, had failed to arrive. One German gentleman, on observing the wickets scattered in all directions by a well-delivered ball, eagerly inquired, "And how much does that count?"'

'The game was to be played upon horses!' What hope, for a people who could not tell cricket from polo? Sporting xenophobia became, to the English, a kind of amusing parlour game: an indulgent and often wildly circuitous exercise in locating the reason why the English themselves were best on earth, and foreigners nowhere. Englishmen everywhere began to wonder aloud, in what were affected to be bemused but tolerant tones, why none but an Englishman was capable of holding a straight bat. Most other countries in the world were subjected to this fastidious, arrogant examination, until – in rapid succession – they disproved their slanderers by effective action in the field. So in the first half of the nineteenth century it was confidently stated that the Australians would never become adept at cricket because their climate rendered wickets too consistently dry; and the Spanish would never take to any sport because their daytime working hours were too long and their peasants too oppressed (as well as their wickets being too dry).

Americans were good at some games, but as they asserted their sporting independence in the second half of the nineteenth century, those games were generally accepted as being games that nobody else (at least, no Englishman) would want to play. In 1907 even the sons of the Celtic fringe, the Welsh, the Irish and the Scots, were deemed by J.E. Vincent to be not much use at the games that mattered because, once their public school term was out, they returned home only 'to shoot, to fish, to swim, to row,' rather than to a village green echoing with the thock of leather on willow.

It was rare that the Celtic allies got it in the neck, of course. Black sportsmen were most regularly (and most recently) patronised as fearful, inadequate footballers and as batsmen who fled from fast bowling – until it was suddenly recognised that their soccer players were clever enough to dominate the English League, and that their cricketers not only played fast bowling better than anybody else, but also bowled the stuff with such regularity, at such a pace, that it was actually unfair to their (white) opponents.

Nation by nation, race by race, the rest of the world dropped out of this parade of Aunt Sallys by queueing up to beat the English and thereby embarrass them into silence, until only the French – who, as we have seen, were there at the beginning – were left. There is something rather touching in the way that the English have clung for two centuries to this single relic of their Georgian and Victorian pretensions: the French person's discomfiture in the presence of a cricket ball.

So, in 1905 'A French Correspondent' to *The Times* would muse: 'The Frenchman gets impatient at waiting his turn to go in, and would like to be either batting or bowling the whole time. In a word, cricket is not sympathetic to the French temperament. There are scarcely a dozen Frenchmen who play the game, and most of them play it abominably.'

In 1953 the same newspaper would wittily editorialise on the topic of Brigadier Gerard reporting home to France that cricket in England was 'a brave pastime, a game for soldiers. Each tries to strike the other with the ball, and it is but a small stick with which you may ward it off. Three sticks behind show the spot beyond which you may not retreat.' And as late as 1980 its columns contained an item on the Lord's Taverners cricket team playing a match on the outskirts of Paris, during which 'small knots of puzzled men gathered round the "guichet" and stared in silence at the footmarks made by the "lanceur" as he hurled the ball at the "batman". They inquired of any English present which of the players was the "maiden".'

By 1980 the French had proved themselves at least in the codes of rugby and association football. But a hundred years earlier the only conceivable exceptions to the useful rule that beyond the watery bounds of Great Britain nobody was any good at games, were to be found in the dominions. 'We believe the cricket ground,' wrote A.I. Shand in 1875, 'to be an appurtenance of our barracks in the Blue Mountains of Jamaica, and sporting contemporaries publish reports of the game from the stations in the Mediterranean to those under the Southern Cross, where garrison teams come in conflict with the civilians who have exiled themselves from home in pursuit of fortune.'

For there, in Jamaica and under the Southern Cross, were nothing less than Britons abroad, racial brothers, men separated perhaps by a waste of ocean and distinguished by superior suntans, but undeniably of the species Britannicus. They were to be found as the governing, fashion-making class in Australasia, in large parts of South Africa, in much of the West Indies and in North America – and they, it was confidently expected, would prove in time to be willing, if not perfectly co-ordinated, overseas playmates for British sportsmen.

They did. Throughout the eighteenth and early nineteenth century the new worlds of America and Australasia proved to be the first great seeding beds of British sport overseas. In 1860 there were no fewer than 10,000 men and boys playing cricket with 500 clubs in 100 cities of the United States of America. It was without doubt those extraordinary statistics – which would be massacred by the American Civil War and the rise of all-American sports such as baseball in its unified aftermath – which attracted an English touring side to North America in 1859.

The All England XI which made landfall at Montreal in September 1859 was the first international select to tour outside the British Isles. They were a team of British professionals, who had first been assembled as a travelling troupe by William Clarke in 1846. They played what could loosely be described as exhibition games. In 1859 they pitted themselves, 11 professionals, against 22 amateur Canadians from the St George's Club of Montreal, and won by eight wickets.

> The twenty-two [reported the *New York Herald*] are laughed at by their friends, who bet two to one on the twenty-two of the St George's Club. The English eleven play splendidly, and it is a perfect picture to see them; but they will find their equals in the twenty-two at Hoboken. There were 6000 people in the ground, and the military band played some fine selections. There were many ladies, military officers, and heads of departments [who were] witnesses to the match . . . The nervousness and run-outs have defeated the Canadians, among whom are several British officers; but it was to be expected when they were pitted against such a magnificent body of cricketers.

They did not, incidentally, despite the *New York Herald*'s promise, find their equals in Hoboken. The All England XI won all five of their matches on tour. Their reputation would fly ahead of them, gilded by the mystique of Empire. Two years later, at the end of 1861, they became the first English cricket team to visit Australia. Cricket may not have been played for so long in the antipodes as in the Americas (it was first recorded in Sydney in 1803), but enthusiasm for the sport was, by the middle of the century, enormous. The Australian Cricket Club had been formed in 1826, and various regional clubs thereafter, and the first inter-colonial match between Victoria and Tasmania had been played in 1851. 'Cricket is now the prevailing amusement of the day,' wrote the *Sydney Gazette* at that time. 'Let no man henceforth set up for sporting character whose name is not enrolled among the "gentleman cricketers" of Sydney. Let no adoring swain hereafter think to "dangle at a lady's apron string" or "feast upon the smiles from partial beauty won", unless he can boast of excellence in handling a bat, or sending up a ball . . .'

And yet the Australians and the Americans watched the arrival of their English counterparts with trembling awe; regarded them as superior beings whose qualifications, as the inventors and eternal guardians of the sport, were beyond the scope of others. If their 'nervousness' in the face of the 'magnificent' Englishmen had defeated the North Americans in 1859, so as late as 1872 the magazine *Land and Water* would be saying of an 'amateur' tour of Toronto and New York (an amateur tour which included the famous professional W.G. Grace):

> The English expected to win, and won; the Canadians probably expected to lose, and lost; so that both sides were well pleased . . . though it would, perhaps, have been more pleasant to all if the colonists had shown more fight . . . There is, perhaps, no real use in these cricketing voyages; they only tell us what we knew before – that there is no such thing as making any handicap which shall bring together first-rate and third-rate cricketers.

(The one glimmer of light on the horizon, concluded *Land and Water* in splendidly scrambled imperial syntax, might have been that the sight of England drubbing Canada could 'teach the rising generation how fields were won, and so to do good service, in the long run, to the "cause of cricket all over the world", as a good old toast, drunk with enthusiasm after a cricket match at many a foreign station from Archangel to Singapore, has it.')

At least the Canadians, after 13 years of the colonial cringe, were coming to terms with it. In the southern summer of 1861–62 the Australians were too busy worrying about how humiliated they might be by the time stumps were drawn. 'Subscriptions are being canvassed,' fretted the *Melbourne Argus*, 'to fetch down the best players from the country districts, so as to organise a team worthy to cope with the [All England] Eleven.

'Practice has within the last week commenced on the Melbourne ground, by having 22 placed in the field – it being expected the Eleven will play against that number – but we fear that a great deal more practice will be required, as at present the fielding is inferior . . . our men will have plenty of work before them, even if they are beaten by a small majority.'

The extent to which this might be considered unnecessary deference may be judged by the fact that just 15 years later, in March 1877, Australia would win the first 'official' Test match against an All England Eleven in Melbourne by 45 runs, and in 1882 the touring Australians would defeat a full-strength England side at the Kennington Oval, London.

In the middle years of the century British athletes were widely regarded as internationally pre-eminent partly because they advertised themselves as such, partly because they were playing the games of their own devising, partly because they actually were still largely untested and undefeated, and partly because for many decades they had controlled and ordered these sports themselves, through that unique and seminal creation of the British bourgeois intelligence: the club. If they were not at first much interested in organising sport for foreigners, the British were at an early date fascinated by the process of organising sport for one another. And because of the British sporting club, people from overseas who contested the pick of those venerable institutions came to feel rather like 13-year-olds taking on a team of games teachers. The students might have fitness, ability and motivation, but they knew in their sinking hearts that they would never be allowed to win.

Which was the oldest sports club? If we exclude momentarily the apparently unique claim of Southampton to have hosted a society of bowlers in the thirteenth century, and if we broaden the definition to include associations of men drawn together by vocational necessity, or by regal command, as much as by recreational interest, and if we agree for the nonce to overlook the requirement of a written constitution – those are all sizeable ifs, but we may live with them – then the archers seem to have it. Archery itself is almost as old as humanity, and it is possible that at a relatively early stage men began to shoot arrows for play as well as for food. It would therefore be nonsensical for Britain to claim the invention of this sport, but . . .

But in 1252 the Statute of Westminster made it compulsory for every English male aged between 15 and 60 years to own a bow which was at least the same length as he was tall, and to practise with it regularly. This piece of legislation resulted in a national aptitude for archery which was probably without precedent, and may not since have been equalled elsewhere in the world. An authority of the time claimed that: 'A first-rate English archer who, in a single minute, was unable to draw and discharge his bow 12 times with a range of 240 yards, and who in those 12 shots once missed his man, was very lightly dismissed.'

No twentieth-century champion of the international archery circuit would be assured of hitting a man-sized target 240 yards away 12 times in 60 seconds. Those superb longbowmen of the Middle Ages completed two military victories which became part of English legend. On 26 August 1346, 6,000 of them faced 15,000 Genoese crossbowmen on a hillside at Crécy-en-Ponthieu in north-western France. By midnight the Genoese and their French employers had been routed. The lesson was quickly learned. In 1363 another edict insisted that archery practice should replace football, handball and cockfighting as a holy day pursuit – a piece of legislation which ensured among other things that for many centuries archery was the only sport which was legally practiced on the Sabbath. Nobody over the age of 24 was allowed to shoot at any target which was less than 220 yards from the bowman. Fifty years after that, at Agincourt in 1415, 5,000 English archers slaughtered the better part of 25,000 French troops. The British cult of archery had produced so devastating a military machine that it not only kept the country free from any threat of invasion, but it seemed to be able to conquer neighbouring lands with a tiny expeditionary force. It also, incidentally, introduced to the world a surviving feature of British common invective. Whenever the French captured an enemy longbowman they cut off the two forefingers of his right hand. As a result, the uncaptured archers took to waving their intact forefingers aloft at the French during battle, displaying a massed V-sign after each deadly volley of arrows . . .

In that short century, the image of the accomplished, irrepressible British longbowman was engraved on the folk memory of the nation. It would still be there at the end of the millennium, six centuries after those astonishing archers had won their last momentous victory. It was no accident that more than 500 years after the end of the Hundred Years' War, a Rule of Shooting of the Grand National Archery Society insisted that all competitors should wear dark grass-green jackets and white or buff trousers, in conscious homage to the uniform of the bowmen who served under Edward III and Henry V.

The Statute of Winchester was re-enacted in 1512, with the fresh insistence that all boys should be taught archery from the age of seven years. But the ascendency of the gun as a weapon of war steadily subdued the demands of government on the archers of England and Wales, and by the sixteenth century archery had become as much of a recreational pursuit – a sport, it must be said – as a footsoldier's craft.

And then came the first societies, the first brotherhoods of this historic and honourable calling. In the independent nation of Scotland, towards the end of the reign of James III in 1483, the Society of Kilwinning Archers was formed. In a country in which the bow had never been of great military importance, it was almost from the beginning a recreational society, and by the close of the twentieth century it was probably the oldest sports club still extant in the world – although it apparently fell moribund during the Reformation, and had to be reconstituted in 1688. Its most celebrated test of skill, in the fifteenth century and for five hundred years after, was the shooting of the papingo, or popinjay. The popinjay was traditionally a wooden parrot on a stick. It apparently derived from an incident in Virgil's *Aeneid* in which the eponymous hero Aeneas, who was travelling in Sicily, observed archers shooting at a tethered dove. One bowman missed the bird but shot through its bindings. At Kilwinning the tethered dove was replaced by a carved parrot which was erected on the roof of the abbey, and which competitors had to knock from its perch.

In England the Guild of the Fraternity of St George was incorporated in 1537, and it arranged large archery shoots (3,000 bowmen are reported as having gathered under its wing at Hodgson's Field, London, in 1583). But the same historical imperatives which had encouraged the development in England of arguably the greatest number of the most accomplished archers ever assembled anywhere on earth, were by then working against the bow and arrow. Following the defeat of the Spanish Armada in 1588 Queen Elizabeth I was given a personal bodyguard of archers, named the Royal Artillery Company, whose members were chosen from the Fraternity of St George. But in 1595 the Artillery Company was instructed by Privy Council to replace all its bows with muskets. It would be re-formed a century later, in 1676, as the Royal Company of Archers, by which time its function was almost entirely recreational.

(It is possible that the longbow was retired prematurely from organised warfare in most of Europe. With less than 3,000 men the Marquis of Montrose defeated a superior force of 7,000 Covenanters at Tippermuir in 1644, using bowmen as his artillery. In skilled hands the bow was more accurate than the musket at ranges of greater than

100 yards until the middle of the nineteenth century; and in May 1940 it was reported with great glee in England that a member of the British Expeditionary Force on the continent of Europe had killed a German soldier with an arrow fired from a bow. In much of the rest of the world, in America, Africa and Asia, indigenous people would continue to use the bow and arrow as a useful, if not entirely effective, weapon of resistance against European colonials until well into the twentieth century.)

The disciplines of war transferred comfortably to sporting competition. Archers of the seventeenth and eighteenth centuries shot at the clout, a large circular straw mark placed 160–240 yards away; or at a smaller paper disc on a butt 100–140 yards away; or at loosely ranged targets over undulating ground – which discipline, known as field archery, was still a part of the World Championships in the twentieth century.

And the clubs and societies proliferated. In 1781 the eccentric founder-collector of the Leverian Museum, Sir Ashton Lever, decided that archery was good therapy for the infirm, and took time off from gathering shells, fossils and 'savage costumes' to form the Toxophilite Society. This important body shortly gained the patronage of the Prince Regent, the future George IV, and became the Royal Toxophilite Society. Prince George is credited, how fairly we do not know, with the invention of the modern standardised target. It was four feet in diameter; its centre circle was gold, the next ring was red, the next one blue, the next one black, and the outer circle was white. They scored nine, seven, five, three, and one points respectively; and they were shot at over three distances: 100, 80, and 60 yards. The scoring system became known as the 'Prince's Reckoning', and the ranges the 'Prince's Lengths'. In August 1844 this legislation was applied at the first British Archery Championships in York, and the sport of modern competitive archery was established. The Grand National Archery Society, which would become the British governing body and the first national legislative council for the sport anywhere in the world, was formed in 1861.

It had a thriving sport to administer. By the end of the eighteenth century there were some 20 archery societies at large in Great Britain. Unlike many of the sporting bodies which would follow them, they were nicely egalitarian associations: the Royal British Bowmen admitted women as shooting members in 1787, and the others quickly followed. Women were not allowed to compete in the first National Championships, but just 12 months later, in 1845, they were welcomed to the butts. And by the time of the third Olympic Games in 1904, archery was a mixed sport. The game suited Edwardian women, in a way which it would be idle and wrong-headed to dismiss. 'There is no violent exertion about it,' wrote a female contributor to the *Brighton Season* in 1906, 'no undue amount of exposure. You can stroll between the targets under your sunshade; and the correct attitudes for shooting are absolutely graceful . . .'

We are allowed some glimpses into the high summer days of these archery clubs. They were, by the time of Victoria, genteel upper middle-class institutions. The Archers of the Nene in Northamptonshire had 14 clergymen, two army officers and five ladies among their 23 members. The Brighton and Hove Archers contained 40 women and just 20 men, shooting on four mornings a week in the grounds of a local private house. John O'Gaunt's Bowmen, who first assembled in Lancaster in 1788, were composed by the 1840s of gentry, clergymen, surgeons and merchants, many of whom were also members of the local rowing and cricket clubs.

Snooty, snobbish, exclusive of the lower classes if not of women, the archery associations which had flourished in Britain since the seventeenth century and which blossomed in the nineteenth, had nonetheless one great achievement: they knocked the sport into order and into an exportable shape. In this they were genuine precursors of all the other imperial games. When a London-born publican named Wilbraham F.E. Liarchet decided to offer his patrons archery lessons at his Brighton Pier Hotel in the colony of Victoria, Australia, in the 1840s, he was able to import to the dominion a respectable set of established rules, as well as targets, bows and arrows. These regulations, transferred intact from the mother country, became in 1856 the code of the first major archery competition to be held in Australia – just as in 1828 they had been holy writ to the pioneering United Bowmen of Philadelphia. In 1878 they would guide the hands of the Chicagoan organisers of the first United States National Archery Championships; and in 1900 they would serve as the basis for archery competitions to be introduced to the second Olympic Games. The sport's first international ruling body, the Fédération Internationale de Tir à l'Arc, was established in 1931, at the time of the first World Championships in Warsaw. Its ancestry was neither French nor Polish. It owed its constitution and its rulebook to the likes of Sir Ashton Lever and his patron the Prince Regent; it owed its disciplines to the clouts, butts and field archery of eighteenth-century Britain, and to the Prince's Reckoning of the Royal Toxophilites.

In such ways were the early sporting clubs of Great Britain influential beyond their dreams or desires. They did not establish themselves in order to colonise their recreations, but once they had formed they set an example which their overseas brethren found impossible to ignore. Armed with their codes, their constitutions, their stopwatches, statistics and record books, they simply invited emulation.

So great games and little games, some indigenous to Great Britain and others not, were cast in a mould of Georgian and Victorian devising. If the first sailing association was the Royal Cork Yacht Club in 1720, it was soon mimicked by others. As with skating and archery, nobody could assert that the British invented sailing, but they invented the modern sailing club – and in doing so, they established not only the basic international form of the sport, but also its social pretensions. They gave it order, and they gave it airs and graces. To many who took up the game overseas, the social pretensions, airs and graces were equally as attractive as the rulebook.

The tone was set in Britain. The Royal Yacht Squadron, which was formed in 1815, turned up its aristocratic nose for many years at the very idea of yacht-racing. The Royal Welsh Yacht Club, whose constitution was first penned in Caernarvon in 1847, barred from its waters any boat which had been used for trade or charter; banned the subjects of politics and religion from its club meetings; insisted upon an arcane distinction between three different shades of blue jacket for the three varieties of club events ('dress, undress and dinner dress'); and – naturally – adopted the black ball system of anonymous rejection of undesirable applicants. The ability to sail well had absolutely nothing to do with membership of these societies.

Unpleasant attitudes and patterns of behaviour were nursed in such institutions, which would be repeated throughout much of the rest of British sport, and which would lead to its serious debilitation. In yachting, the stultifying effects of exclusivity and arrogance were, as it happened, made obvious at an early date.

The first major international yacht race took place in 1851. It was part of the imperial festivities which surrounded the Great Exhibition of that year. The race took the familiar shape of a run out of Cowes around the Isle of Wight. Fourteen British boats were involved, and one representative from the New York Yacht Club: the *America*. A Hundred Guineas Cup was put up, but the result was of course a foregone conclusion. Competitive sailing was, in 1851, hardly known of in the USA. The New York Yacht Club was the first and only such fraternity in the New World, and it was just seven years old.

The *America* won the race. It returned with its trophy to the New York Yacht Club, and offered it, newly christened the America's Cup, for intermittent challenge from foreign sailors. No boat from Britain, which was for the best part of a century after 1851 the greatest maritime power in the world, ever won back the America's Cup. British yacht clubs did not, after all, contain the finest or even a selection of the most capable sailors in the country. The Americans may have turned their emerging yacht clubs into simulacra of the British model, but they could never properly imitate the stuffy, class-bound incompetence of the real thing. Despite the oceans of money pumped into British forays across the Atlantic by the likes of tradesman millionaire Sir Thomas Lipton (of whose efforts on the water, it was recounted with sniggers around Cowes and Henley, and Caernarvon, Kaiser Wilhelm II wondered: 'Why does the Prince of Wales go yachting with his grocer?') the America's Cup stayed defiantly American for 132 years – until it was finally snatched from the NYYC in 1983 by an Australian competitor from the Royal Perth Yacht Club. Australia had not been blessed with so much as a single yacht club until 1856, when the Victorian Yacht Club was born; with the Australian Yacht Squadron (1862) hard astern. Each of these institutions would shortly be allowed to prefix itself with the word 'Royal', which may contain some small but significant part of the reason why it took their normally athletic and egalitarian countrymen more than a hundred years to win the America's Cup.

Such trifling setbacks as having 14 of their best sailing boats beaten by a single American did not deter the British. Mostly, they chose simply to follow the lead of the Royal Yacht Squadron and ignore the America's Cup and, by definition, the rest of the sailing world. By refusing to repeat the ignominy of 1851, they might be able to obscure its memory. This sad pretence – that because, as the originator, one obviously is the best in the world, one does not have to prove it – would be repeated in other sports, with equally diminishing results.

But that did not prevent them from assuming that their local dispensation would be internationally respected. Extraordinarily, the assumption was often correct, not least because the British, with all their finely printed rule books and constitutions, were frequently the only people who were actually bothered to try to impose global standards. Their first attempt to whip yachting into line came on 1

June 1868, when the Royal Victoria Yacht Club organised a 'Yacht-ing Congress'. Painstaking work by a duly appointed sub-committee of this Congress resulted in the publication of a pamphlet which detailed all the different rules which applied at all of the existing yacht clubs. Armed with this stultifying document, the Yachting Congress met again on 4 March 1869, and adopted a draft of new international racing rules. When exposed to criticism in the press, however, the new rules were holed below the waterline. They quickly sank, taking down with them the shortlived Yachting Congress.

Perhaps a royal finger in the legislative pie was essential. Most of the yachting clubs in Britain and in the dominions (although not in the USA) were delightedly designated Royal. Queen Victoria's eldest son, HRH Albert Edward, the Prince of Wales, was commodore of both the Royal Thames Yacht Club and the Royal Yacht Squadron. He brought the two of them together with the New Thames Yacht Club in 1881 to form the Yacht Racing Association, which applied a standard set of yachting rules to British waters. Twenty-five years later, in 1906, the secretary of the YRA, Major Brooke Heckstall–Smith, convened a conference in London which resulted in the formation of the International Yacht Racing Union. And 23 years after that, in 1929, the Americans courteously agreed to contain their own rules within the legislation of the IYRU. The International Yacht Racing Union, a body which rose from British waters at a time when British yachtsmen were patently far from being the best in the world, would become the unchallenged arbiter of global competitive sailing. It would be recognised as such by the Olympic committee and by 115 affiliated nations, and would organise a string of major contests. It would never, of course, get its hands on the America's Cup.

Such was the power of association; in such ways did the British promulgate overseas their own visions of organised sport.

They were engaged for a century and more in an exercise which, as nobody else had thought to do it before, was absolutely engrossing. They were slapping the world's recreation into shape. It was a truly imperial exercise, the kind of hobby which passed perfectly the leisure hours in between annexing fresh parts of the Indian sub-continent and pacifying the Gilbert and Ellice Islands, and the more they practised at it, the better they got. It was not, in its early decades, part of any magnificent plan to scatter the world with British spec-tator sports. It was just that disorganised sports became increasingly offensive to the British eye. They were so . . . unnecessary. Not one of them was safe. Before long, no game could be hidden from the stern, inquiring gaze of a Victorian legislator . . .

Edith Somerville and Martin Ross (the latter being the pen-name of Violet Florence Martin) of the literary partnership Somerville and Ross came from Anglo-Irish families in County Cork and Galway. They published their stories of a residential magistrate, *The Irish R.M.*, between 1899 and 1908. The tales were undoubtedly drawn from life: Somerville, who was the main partner, was immersed in the county life of Castletownshead in Cork.

So she knew all about the old Celtic amusement of road bowls. This activity had been commonplace for centuries throughout the western fringes of Britain. It may have been the grimy disreputable grandfather of the sport which Francis Drake and John Hawkins enjoyed on Plymouth Hoe while waiting for the tide to turn on the Spanish Armada; that more genteel game which apparently first led the Georgian British into a preoccupation with trimming their lawns. It was a simple, uncouth thing, this road bowls. For its last two or three centuries of life it was heavily involved with gambling, because its elementary form was most suited to a straightforward bet. At the end of the nineteenth century, however, it became one of the very few sports ever to be criminalised in Great Britain and Ireland. That was not ostensibly because of its unsavoury associations, but rather because road bowls – which simply called upon one participant to propel a heavy metal ball (cannon-shot, and even stones were occasionally used) farther than his opponent along a stretch of highway with a limited number of shots – was perceived as being a danger to late-Victorian traffic.

When Somerville and Ross sent their narrator and leading man, the residential magistrate Major Sinclair Yeates, on a trip into the hills of Cork to confront a suspected criminal, they chose to leave us with a last glimpse of this ancient, fugitive game. Major Yeates's horse, the Quaker, was pulling him along in a small carriage . . .

> I got out, and walked up the hill, stiffly, because the cramp of the covered car was in my legs. Stiff though I was, I had outpaced the Quaker, and was near the top of the hill, when something that was apparently a brown croquet–ball rolled swiftly round the bend above me, charged into the rock wall of the cutting with a clang, and came on down the hill with a weight and venom unknown to croquet–balls. It sped past me, missed the Quaker by

an uncommonly near shave, and went on its way, hotly pursued by two dogs, who, in the next twenty yards, discovered with horror that it was made of iron, a fact of which I was already aware.

I have always been as lenient as the law, and other circumstances, would allow towards the illegal game of 'bowling'. It consists in bowling an iron ball along a road, the object being to cover the greatest possible distance in a given number of bowls. It demands considerable strength and skill, and it is played with a zest much enhanced by its illegality and by its facilities as a medium for betting. The law forbids it, on account of its danger to the unsuspecting wayfarer, in consideration of which a scout is usually posted ahead to signal the approach of the police, and to give warning to passers-by.

This was without doubt an antique diversion. Whether it was the true progenitor of the flat and crown-green bowls which would captivate respectable Britain may be in question. There is evidence that the Celts, who were after all in Britain before the Anglo-Normans, simply continued to prefer their version of bowls to the imported variety. The Italians, Swiss, Germans and Basques all played a form of bowls which may have been carried into Britain by the Normans. It favoured not distance but accuracy: as it evolved in medieval England its purpose became to strike either a fixed single object such as another, smaller wood known as a half bowl, or to knock over a group of skittles or ninepins. During the reign of Henry IV (1399–1415) bowling lanes were built on to the side of the dining rooms of Old Northumberland House, and in 1455 an indoor, covered bowling alley was built specifically to house the sport in London. Both of these developments would have been, almost without doubt, homes for the adult games of skittles or ninepins.

And from those elementary beginnings another small recreation of old England took a curious global peregrination. Bowling reached North America at a very early date. It has been suggested that the ships of Henry Hudson carried a wooden ball and skittles when the explorer ascended the Hudson River to Albany in 1609. Ninepins became popular in the New World and, as in the Old, they achieved a bad reputation through being played in the grounds of public houses and being linked to betting. So bad a reputation did they acquire, in fact, that in the 1840s the state legislature of Connecticut outlawed ninepin bowling.

Devotees of the game circumnavigated this misfortune by adding a tenth skittle. Tenpin bowling flourished in the United States, alongside its siblings fivepins, duckpins and candlepins. In 1895 the American Bowling Congress formed itself in New York to standardise the rules. The sport boomed after the Second World War, when 'glamorous new air-conditioned, fully serviced alleys were built; automatic pinsetting machines replaced the grubby tip-grabbing pinboys, and rock'n'roll music was piped throughout the glittering gymnasia. By the end of the 1950s the ABC, with a registered three-and-a-half million male competitive bowlers alone, was describing itself as 'the world's largest participation sports organisation'. And also in the 1950s a series of American-model bowling halls were introduced to Britain. They were in fact nothing more or less than direct descendants of those bowling alleys of fifteenth-century London, but few people recognised them as such. Like base ball and ice hockey, ninepins and skittles returned as foreigners to the home which they had left 350 years earlier.

The adherents of Southampton Town Bowling Club back in the thirteenth century were probably not playing alley bowls with skittles or ninepins, but lawn bowls with full and half woods. Despite its patriotic associations with Drake and Hawkins, Hudson and Henry VIII, by the nineteenth century even lawn bowls had fallen out of favour with the administrative classes of England. They frowned upon its reputation. They did not outlaw the game, as they outlawed the old Celtic road bowls, but they eschewed it and seemed likely to deprive it even of the blessing of a constitution, until the Scots and the Australians stepped in.

A Glaswegian solicitor first wrote down some rules for flat green bowling in 1849, and a series of respectable Scottish clubs were built upon his efforts. Four years earlier there had been established at least two, and possibly three, bowling greens in Australasia: in Tasmania, New South Wales, and Norfolk Island. These antipodean lawns were routinely established in the grounds of public houses, which attracted less opprobrium in the colonies than in Victorian Britain. 'Thomas Shaw,' announced one advertisement, 'of the Woolpack Inn, Parramatta Road, has much pleasure in announcing to his numerous patrons, Friends and the Sporting Gentlemen of Sydney and its environs that he has just completed . . . a full-sized, beautifully turfed bowling green . . . [He] confidently looks forward to being honoured by a large meeting of gentlemen, especially amateurs in the true old English game.'

The Melbourne Bowling Club was established in 1864, and the New South Wales Bowling Association in 1880. The Scottish Bowling Association, the first in Britain, was not formed until 1892. Bowls became a major Australian sport – a century after the birth of the New South Wales Bowling Association, the country would contain almost 4,500 clubs and half a million bowlers of both sexes. They amounted to no less than 43 per cent of the world's bowling population. The Australians also became the first country to send an international bowling team on tour, when several of their players visited England and Scotland in the wake of a touring cricket side in 1899.

But immediately after this, in a fascinating instance of imperial pretension, the English reasserted their claim. No sooner had the Australians departed than an Imperial Bowling Association was formed in London. A sportsman more famous for his prowess at cricket, the 52-year-old Dr W.G. Grace, displayed an interest in bowls, and in 1901 he launched a London Counties Association – which was affiliated to the Scottish Bowling Association. Very quickly, between the June of 1903 and the April of 1904, England, Ireland and Wales established their own national Bowling Associations, and a home international series was begun.

The dominions were not entirely forgotten. A New Zealand team followed the Australians to Britain in 1901, and a selection of Canadians in 1904. But the international focus of the sport had been, once more, lifted from the grasp of the Britons abroad as firmly as a toy being confiscated from a child. In 1905 the Imperial Bowling Association became the International Bowling Board. It established, as it would continue to do, the rules of the game. Under its auspices a regular series of international fixtures were arranged. Canadian bowlers visited Britain in 1908, 1912 and 1924; Britons went to Canada in 1906, 1910, 1921 and 1927. Visits were exchanged with the South Africans in 1922 and 1926; with New Zealand in 1907, 1921, 1925 and 1926; and with Australia in 1912, 1922 and 1925.

And yet not until June 1928 was the constitution of the International Bowling Board amended to permit the representatives of Australia, Canada, New Zealand and South Africa to be admitted as members – and even then, when the children from the colonies were allowed just one seat apiece at the high table, the four home countries increased their own allocation from two each to three. The ensuing story makes an enchanting fable of the efforts of perfidious Albion to retain and promote a sporting empire while its international commercial and military stock slumped.

A year later, in 1929, it was decided to give the restless dominions an extra seat on the board, thereby apparently fixing the difference at just one seat. But, in the words of the IBB's own official historian, 'the extra representative had to be chosen from one of the Home Associations'. Thus, Australia's new international officer was an Englishman, New Zealand's was Welsh, Canada's Scottish, and South Africa was fronted by an additional member of the Irish Bowling Association.

This was clearly far from perfect, and the home countries knew it. In 1937 they actually voted their portion up to four seats apiece, while leaving the cousins at two (one of whom was, of course, a Briton or an Irishman). There were therefore, at the close of that year, 20 Britons on the committee of the International Bowling Board and just four men from the dominions. Nine years earlier, before the board had apparently decided to attempt some parity, the ratio had been merely 12 to four.

'The disparity in representation on the board,' reads the IBB's official history in nicely judged words, 'between the Home Countries with four representatives and the others with only two, gave rise to resentment and in 1939 the Australian Bowling Council submitted a motion to the International Bowling Board to amend the Constitution so that each member country should have only two representatives.'

The Australian motion was defeated. Extraordinarily, it was not until 1952, when each country was permitted four members, that equality was established on the International Bowling Board between Great Britain and its bowling colonies.

It was only partly a matter of control. There were certainly cynical manoeuvres involved in keeping the game in British hands, but they were not entirely prompted by a lust for power. The fact was that the Victorian British – and most men who sat on the International Bowling Board before the Second World War would have been born and raised in the previous century – actually did believe that, just as they had been sent in God's image to rule India, so they were also divinely intended to control the international development of lawn bowls. They were hearing still a long, loud echo from the end of the eighteenth century; a call which insisted that only the British were competent to play and to govern sport, and that between the British at Home and the British Abroad, it was better to back the British at Home. There was no particular offence intended to the others, it was just that, well . . . the British at home understood about these things. It was something in the air; something in the water; something in the incorruptible meadows of the English countryside; something which was lost even to Britons, after a certain amount of time beneath the tropical sun. Others may have been playing some games for as long or even longer, but who else had made them neat and tidy and comprehensible from Melbourne to Manchester?

Some sports were so old and so widespread, however, that it was not only impossible for even the British to claim their origination; it would also prove difficult to establish for them an international legislative body based in London. In ancient contests such as horse-racing and boxing, the British influence was of necessity more subtle. It was, for all that, pervasive; not least because horse racing developed across the English-speaking world as a spectator sport and as a gambling institution in the years when the greatest part of the English-speaking world was British in custom and British in government. Britons at home and Britons abroad created the modern turf.

The first Gold Cup was run at Newmarket in 1634. Three decades later, in 1665, the first circular racetrack was built in the American colonies. It was laid out at Hempstead plain on Long Island, and it was named Newmarket. The British American colonists took to horseracing like hogs at a trough. The eighteenth-century Virginian landowner William Byrd II laid out a circular racetrack on his Westover estate, as part of the same colonial impulse which made him turn also to laying a bowling green, and to playing cricket, ninepins, skittles and billiards. These people were, after all, simply Britons abroad. Some of them might later rebel against the government of George III, but just as their language was always and irrevocably English, just as they perceived themselves as springing from the British corner of high European culture, so their recreations would also be Anglo-Saxon and Celtic.

They clung like castaways to such memories of the mother country. 'This is to give notice,' announced the *Boston Gazette* in 1725, 'to all gentlemen and others that there is to be Thirty Pounds in money run for . . . by Six Horses, Mares or Geldings, Two miles to carry 9 stone Weight, the Standard to be 14 hands high . . . the 3 first Horses to run a second Heat.'

Such sophistication in distance, handicapping and the ordering of heats indicate that racing in America lagged hardly at all behind racing in Great Britain. In 1730 the first thoroughbred Arabian stallion was introduced to America from England, and 13 years after that, in 1743, the Maryland Jockey Club was formed at Annapolis.

The Maryland Jockey Club was actually nine years ahead of its great English equivalent. A jockey, in the English-speaking world of the seventeenth and eighteenth century, did not merely mean a rider of racing horses. A jockey was then anyone who managed horses, or who had to do with them in any way. And when a jockey club was established at Newmarket in England in 1752 it was not thought necessary to distinguish it geographically, as the Newmarket Jockey Club, or the English Jockey Club, or the British Jockey Club, or even as the Imperial Jockey Club. It was and ever would be, in haughty disregard of its overseas relatives, the Jockey Club. The jockeys of the Jockey Club at its formation in 1752 were not small wiry men with bandy legs, but oligarchic aristocrats eager to exercise the same influence over their preferred recreation as they already exercised over their lands, their tenants, and the men under their military command. In achieving this ambition they succeeded in turning the Newmarket Jockey Club, rather than its predecessor in Annapolis, if not into an international governing body (they were, we must recall, Georgians, and as such were less concerned with governing internationally than with governing in the sceptr'd isle), then unarguably into the most celebrated and imitated racing organisation in the world – and, equally certainly, the institution which moulded in its own image the massive investment concern that the twentieth century racetrack would become.

Look at them. William George Frederick Cavendish, Lord George Bentinck, statesman and private secretary to the foreign secretary George Canning – Bentinck, who, when he was not fighting Peel's corn laws, was himself riding in races at Goodwood. Bentinck, whom the Jockey Club itself would eulogise as the man whose 'administrative gifts instigated the organisation of race meetings on recognisably modern lines'.

Or Albert Edward Harry Mayer Archibald Primrose, the sixth Lord Rosebery, who inherited an extraordinary stables from his statesman father (the fifth Lord Rosebery had three times won the Derby) and became himself the president of the Surrey Cricket Club and of the MCC, and who won two Derbies and was a lifelong member of the Jockey Club. The sixth Lord Rosebery, who is perhaps not as well celebrated as he deserves to be for a sentence which speaks volumes. When asked how a certain development in horseracing would be received by the public, Albert Primrose replied: 'The public don't count.'

Or Admiral Henry John Rous, the Conservative MP and Lord of the Admiralty who put his position as steward of the Jockey Club above all others; Rous, who in the early decades of the nineteenth century 'shaped the British racing system in such a manner that he left the imprint of his ideas and personality not only on Turf institutions, but also on the British thoroughbred itself.'

Or the Earl of Glasgow, who took it upon himself in the nineteenth century to blackball a certain unfortunate Colonel Forester on each occasion that the latter put himself up for the Jockey Club, once chartering a special train from Scotland to ensure his prompt arrival at the club's London headquarters at voting hour.

This was in no way a democratic, accountable group of men. Until 1835 they refused even to make public a list of members. Not until 1929 was a non-hereditary peer elected to the Jockey Club (Lord Glanely had purchased his title from Lloyd George for £100,000). In 1977 the 225-year-old body admitted its first woman: the Countess of Halifax. Its stated policy was and remains to 'elect its own members from those who are interested in racing and whom members consider suitable to exercise authority and jurisdiction in such matters.' In terms purely of exclusivity it was akin to all of its contemporaries in the yachting world, and for similar reasons: the ownership of racehorses was as expensive a commitment as was the ownership of a racing yacht. If there was a difference between the two it was slight, and was to be found in the extraordinary mystique of the horse: that symbol for centuries past of the warrior knight; of the man born to conquer and rule; of the mailed and liveried ancestors, long gone but never forgotten, of Lords Bentinck, Rosebery and Glasgow.

But they invented modern horseracing. They took a stranglehold on the British fancy, and they used it to develop all of the panoply of the turf and all of the seedy glitter of a day at the races, as it would be experienced from Johannesburg to Kentucky to Hong Kong. From the beginning, horseracing was developed in Britain not so much for the riders as for the owners, who were gambling spectators rather than participants, and so horseracing, which was probably the last and the greatest of antiquity's entertainments, became also the first enormous spectator sport that the modern world had seen.

The races were big, crude, brash and corrupt, and an enormous attraction. 'This English dissipation,' read a petition to the United

States' grand jury against the building of a new racecourse in Philadelphia in 1802, a petition which was signed by 2,700 productive citizens . . .

'This English dissipation of horseracing may be agreeable to a few idle landed gentlemen, who bestow more care in training their horses than educating their children, and it may be amusing to British mercantile agents, and a few landed characters in Philadelphia; but it is in the greatest degree injurious to the mechanical and manufacturing interest, and will tend to our ruin if the nuisance is not removed by your patriot exertions.'

Opposing petitions have rarely disturbed the even tenor of popular recreation. In 1830 there were 56 race meetings for thoroughbred horses in the United States; by 1839 there were 130. In 1836 it was estimated that the US racehorse trading market amounted to $500,000. In 1823 70,000 people turned up at the Union Racecourse on Long Island to watch the champion of the northern states, Eclipse, beat the champion of the south, Sir Henry, for a purse of $20,000. 'For several days before the race,' reported *Niles' Weekly Register*, 'the stages and steamboats arriving at New York were burthened with anxious passengers – many of whom, no doubt, had travelled 500 miles to witness the important contest of speed! It was estimated that not less than 20,000 strangers were in the city of New York – all the hotels, inns, taverns and boarding houses were jammed with people from the bottom to the top, and on the day of the race, the city was deserted.'

The British took this 'English dissipation' with them to India, of course, where they built the biggest racecourse in the world at Calcutta, and the smallest one at Darjeeling. They took it to Ireland, where the old game of steeplechasing, which derived from young English bloods racing over hedge and stream towards a distant church tower, was introduced in 1752, and where they built a splendid arena named the Curragh. They built a racecourse high in the hill station of Simla, and one in the middle of the city of Colombo. When in 1889 a detachment of the Royal Horse Guards arrived at the kraal of the Ndebele King Lobengula of Mashonaland in order to prepare the way for the first detachment of Cecil Rhodes's Pioneer Column into Zimbabwe, the cavalry officers promptly organised in this hostile place a horse race around the extensive walls of Lobengula's redoubt. Two of their races were christened there and then the Zambesi Handicap and the Bulawayo Plate. The ill-fated British expeditionary force had no sooner arrived in Afghanistan in 1839, than it had organised steeplechases and flat races (and cricket, and rugby, and skating) on the outer bounds of Kabul.

Happy Valley in the colony of Hong Kong was a pretty glen over-looking Victoria Harbour from the island hills, which the early colonists found to be an attractive suburb until it proved to be unhealthy to Europeans; after which it was given over to three diverse social amenities: a nest of superior brothels, a number of cemeteries, and a racecourse. The first races were run at Happy Valley in 1846, just five years after a British naval party had first raised the Union Jack three miles away. The early meets were rather like 'a Galway point-to-point', but in 1871 gambling was made illegal in Hong Kong in every area of life other than that of the turf. After that, Happy Valley could not fail. Hong Kong brought together the Victorian colonial British and the Chinese: two of the most committed gambling cultures that the world has known; and in Hong Kong they could bet legally only on the horses. The Royal Hong Kong Jockey Club was formed in 1885, and before the century was out it would be said that Hong Kong 'was ruled by the Jockey Club, the Hongkong and Shanghai Bank, and the Governor – in that order'.

Australian racing ponies were imported into Hong Kong, for horseracing had been commonplace in the antipodes since almost the day of the British arrival there. Australia had never seen a horse before 1788, when the First Fleet unloaded seven thoroughbreds at Sydney Cove. By 1800 there were 200 horses in the colony. In 1810 there were 1,100, and by 1990 Australia had a thoroughbred racehorse population of 80,000. There is evidence of a 'race ground' having existed by the Hawkesbury River near Richmond in 1806, and of an official race meeting organised at Hyde Park in Sydney by officers of the 73rd Regiment between 15 and 19 October 1810. In January 1842 the Australian Jockey Club was founded. Just thirty years after that the first Warrnambool Grand Annual Steeplechase was run. One of the longest, most arduous, and certainly most idiosyncratic of all of the colonial events, it was run over 5,500 metres and 33 fences. In 1909 and 1934 a curious record was set there: no horse finished at Warrnambool. Each one of the 16 starters had either fallen or baulked.

They were mass spectator sports, commonplace to the cities of the world a hundred years later, but novel to the Georgians and the early Victorians. It took a Frenchman to identify and to describe their unique appeal – to give an unforgettable, dispassionate foretaste of a whole world to come. One goes to such events, wrote Hippolyte

Taine after a visit to Epsom on Derby Day in 1861, for one reason only: 'to witness a spectacle'.

There were 200,000 people sharing Epsom Downs with Hippolyte Taine on 28 May 1861.

> The spectacle is interesting only on account of its size. From the top of the Stand the enormous ant-heap swarms, and its din ascends . . . a light mist, charged with sunshine, flits in the distance, and the illuminated air, like a glory, envelops the plain, the heights, the vast area, and all the disorder of the human carnival . . .
>
> A bell rings, and the race is about to begin. The three or four hundred policemen clear the course; the stands are filled, and the meadow in front of them is but a large black patch. We ascend to our places; nothing seems at all imposing. At this distance the crowd is an ant-heap; the horsemen and carriages which move forward and cross each other resemble beetles. May-bugs, large sombre drones on a green cloth. The jockeys in red, in blue, in yellow, in mauve, form a small group apart, like a swarm of butterflies which has alighted. Probably I am wanting in enthusiasm, but I seem to be looking at a game of insects.
>
> Thirty-four run; after three false starts they are off; fifteen or twenty keep together, the others are in small groups, and one sees them moving down the far side of the circuit. To the eye the speed is not very great; it is that of a railway train seen at a distance of half a league – when the carriages look like toy coaches which a child pulls along on a string. For several minutes the brown patch, dotted with red and bright spots, moves steadily over the distant green. It turns: one perceives the first group approach. 'Hats off!' and all heads are uncovered, and everyone rises; a repressed 'hurrah' runs through the stands.
>
> The frigid faces are on fire; brief, nervous gestures suddenly stir the phlegmatic bodies; below, in the betting ring, the agitation is extraordinary – like a general St Vitus's dance; picture a mass of puppets receiving an electric shock, and gesticulating with all their members like mad semaphores. But the most curious spectacle is the human tide which instantly pours forth and rolls over the course behind the runners, like a wave of ink; the black, motionless crowd has suddenly become molten; in a moment it spreads itself over a vast area. The policemen make a

barrier in two or three ranks, using force when necessary to
guard the square to which the jockeys and horses are led.

Hippolyte Taine returned to London in the evening of that May
day in 1861 – the year of the first Melbourne Cup in Australia, and
just two years before the Société des Steeplechases was formed in his
own native country – through crowds of drinking, fighting men. He
saw the people staggering and vomiting and laughing through the
streets of the capital, and observed that nobody chided them, nobody
expressed disgust.

Hippolyte Taine had seen the infancy of industrial sport, in the
cradle of the industrial revolution. On such a sports day, he mused,
'Everything is allowable, it is an outlet for a year of repression.'

CHAPTER FIVE

Britain Rules OK?

Quite apart from the fact that Boxing is a fine sport which calls for a high degree of physical fitness and mental alertness, it is an accomplishment which, above all others, helps a fellow to look after himself should he find himself in an awkward situation. In the bad old days of the Wild West it used to be said that the most lawful communities were those in which every man carried a gun on his hip. More often than not the guns were never used. That was because those who were inclined to start trouble were held in check by the thought that if they did start something, somebody else might finish it.

It is the same with Boxing. Even today there are people about who think they can get what they want by bullying. But it is significant that bullies always seem to avoid picking on the chap who is said to be useful with his fists. You have probably noticed that at school.

The Boy's Book of Sport, Carlton Wallace, 1951

In 1806 an English novelist named Thomas Ashe described in a book titled *Travels in America* a scene which he had witnessed in Wheeling, Virginia. Ashe had found himself in Wheeling on a day when a horserace had caused two-thirds of the town to take the day off work.

The racing ended in arguments and scuffles, and finally in a well-attended fight between a Viriginian and a Kentuckian. They sparred for a while, as Ashe recounted, before the Virginian launched his attack with a lunging blow . . .

'The shock received by the Kentuckyan, and the want of breath, brought him instantly to the ground. The Virginian never lost his hold; like those bats of the South who never quit the subject on which they fasten till they taste blood, he kept his knees in his enemy's body; fixing his claws in his hair, and his thumbs on his eyes, gave them an instantaneous start from their sockets. The sufferer roared aloud, but uttered no complaint.'

Despite having his eyes dangling on stalks over his cheekbones, the uncomplaining man from Kentucky managed to bite off the Virginian's nose, whereupon the Virginian concluded the contest by tearing his opponent's lower lip below his chin. Both men retired to sustained applause.

This, clearly, was a sport in need of legislation. It may or may not have cheered the lacerated Kentuckian to know that across the Atlantic, where the game had been known as boxing since the Middle Ages (boxing was an old English word: the apparently more venerable term 'pugilism' actually entered the language later, from Latin), a set of rules was already in place which limited the numbers of deaths and terrible injuries suffered by those who stood up to fight in front of crowds.

Most early sporting rules were agreed and enforced as much to protect life and limb as to increase the entertainment value of the game. (In the case of boxing, many would argue all down the centuries that the increase of the former was commensurate with the decline of the latter. It was an argument which echoed from the old Roman concern about whether sparing the life of a crippled gladiator did not, after all, diminish the contest.)

Bareknuckle prize-fighting had been commonplace in seventeenth-century Britain, where it was no more than an adjunct of duelling (for many decades prize-fighters would adapt their foot movements and their stances from those of swordsmen). The results of such unlimited, unlegislated battles were frequently so hideous that they disquieted even an enthusiast who lived in the early eighteenth century.

Jack Broughton was born of an impoverished family in 1704, and when he died 84 years later his public esteem was such that he became the first of the few sportsmen or women actually to be buried in Westminster Abbey. Broughton was celebrated chiefly because of his bravery and accomplishments. Having been a 'public bruiser' fighting challengers for pennies out of a booth in Tottenham Court Road, he then joined the soldiery and did not return to boxing until 1742, when he established a 'theatre for pugilism' in Hanway Street, hard by the west end site of his former booth.

Almost immediately, an opponent of Broughton's died from injuries sustained during an unregulated contest. There is little need to recreate these eighteenth-century affairs. They were bare-knuckled; they permitted virtually all effective tactics, strokes, blows, holds or throws; they were fought within a ring of rope or wooden palings; and they went on until one contestant was suing for peace, was unconscious, or was dead.

Jack Broughton decided after the fatality of his own opponent that prize-fighting was in need of some civilisation. It was not a popular decision. Boxers, or pugilists, were then little better than gladiators fighting for the amusement of the Fancy. Broughton's own emporium was closed down in 1750, apparently at the command of his disgusted patron the Duke of Cumberland (who was already known in Scotland as 'Butcher' Cumberland following his brutal suppression of the Jacobite uprising of five years earlier). Broughton was, at the age of 45, fighting one Slack. Cumberland had wagered £10,000 on Broughton beating Slack. Broughton did not do so. Blinded by his own blood, he had staggered bravely on, shouting to his sponsor at ringside: 'I can't see my man, Your Highness. I am blind but not beat. Only place me before him and he shall not gain the day yet.' Slack did gain the day, and Jack Broughton's boxing emporium was finished.

But in 1743, while Jack Broughton was in his pomp and men like 'Butcher' Cumberland were winning small fortunes from his victories, the champion took the opportunity to legislate for the game of boxing. His rules were minimal: their significance lay in the fact that they were rules at all. He made it illegal (or at least, irregular) to hit a fallen opponent, or to hit below the belt. Eye-gouging was outlawed. A boxer who was knocked over was to be allowed 30 seconds' recovery (which incidentally caused greater damage than before, since a clearly damaged fighter now had time to recover). Such a knockdown signalled the end of a round – it was, indeed, the only measurement of a round. And that was about it. But 'Broughton's Code' laid the groundwork for the development of the sport of boxing out of the brutal mêlée of prize-fighting; it set the tone of the sport for the next century, and Broughton's rules were in operation during the first international match.

Too little is known of that contest, for one glaring and disgraceful reason. It was between the great Regency pugilist Tom Cribb of England (who had been called upon to guard the entrance to Westminster Hall at the coronation of George IV, and had performed before the Tsar of Russia), and the American Tom Molineaux. It took place in December 1810 to the north of London. Cribb won in the 39th round. Molineaux, according to an English observer, 'proved himself as courageous a man as ever an adversary contended with . . . [he] astonished everyone, not only by his extraordinary power of hitting, and his gigantic strength, but also by his acquaintance with the science, which was far greater than any had given him credit for'.

By a stroke of good fortune, at least one of the artist brothers George and Isaac Robert Cruikshank were present that day, and they later released an engraving of the event. The first ever international boxing match took place in the countryside. The Fancy stood around or sat in their carriages upon a nearby knoll, while down at ringside the mob bayed and screamed. The ring was, by 1810, a square enclosed by a kind of rustic fence. There were six men in the ring: two seconds for each fighter, urging their champion on; and the two combatants. In the Cruikshanks' engraving, which presumably depicts the 39th round, a grizzled Tom Cribb is delivering a conclusive straight right to the chin of the falling Molineaux.

And there also is depicted the clue to the American's lack of fame in his own country. Tom Molineaux, the 'courageous' scientific boxer, the first to represent the USA in an international bout, was black. Some said that he was a former slave.

It took a further 50 years for another American to sail the Atlantic in pursuit of an English boxing champion, and this time the man was an acceptable shade of pale. John Camel Heenan of West Troy, New York, 'the Benicia Boy', was an Irish-American. The two great strands of ethnicity among early American boxing heroes were thereby represented in their first two international challengers.

Heenan went in search of Tom Sayers, a bricklayer from Pimlico. They met up at Farnborough Common in Hampshire in 1860, in the second international boxing match. This time, America took notice. 'With the mass of people,' declared *The New York Times*, 'it is now the great topic of speculation . . . throwing completely into shade all political themes and everything else which can afford to wait.'

The Sayers–Heenan fight was also one of the last great prize-fights to be played out under Broughton's rules: those elementary restrictions which had dominated boxing for a hundred years, and had helped to turn it – on both sides of the Atlantic – from a bloody maul into a semi-house-trained sport. 'Everything was conducted according to superstitiously observed rules,' wrote one journalist after having watched Sayers fight Heenan in 1860. '[There were] almost as many ceremonies as at the Coronation.'

But not enough 'superstitiously observed rules' to satisfy the Hampshire constabulary, who intervened to stop the fight in the 42nd round. The match was declared a draw. Tom Sayers never fought again. He died five years later, at the age of 39. In 1867, two years after his death, the first Marquis of Queensberry championships featuring heavy, middle and lightweight boxers were launched in London under the patronage of Oscar Wilde's persecutor, Sir John Sholto Douglas.

The 'Queensberry Rules' were truly revolutionary, and were clearly designed to keep alive a sport whose ferocious contests were no longer acceptable to the police or to the respectable public even under Jack Broughton's restrictions. They were not, in fact, designed by John Douglas, the Marquis of Queensberry, but by a Welshman named John Graham Chambers. Chambers, even more than Broughton, civilised boxing. The difference between his bouts and the fearful 42-round exhibitions which brought to an end the careers of such as Tom Sayers, was enormous. Jack Broughton had set out a century earlier to reduce the number of people dying in the boxing ring; John Chambers aimed to offer victory in the ring not just to the survivor, but to the most stylish fighter.

Chambers got the Marquis of Queensberry to attach his name to three trophies to be fought for at the three different weights of light, middle and heavy. All contests were gloved. Just three timed rounds of three minutes each were endured, after which, if a ten-second knock-out had not been achieved, judges awarded points as much for balance, grace and cunning as for strength.

The gentlemanly amateurs of the late-Victorian period adopted the sport and did the rest. Boxing would never be the same again. The old game died hard, however. The Pelican Club, which was formed in 1887 by a couple of kenspeckle characters named William 'The Shifter' Goldberg and Ernest 'Swears' Wells, was a late throwback to the riotous heyday of the Regency. The Pelican Club was brought to its knees at a bareknuckle fight by its most infamous member.

The millionaire George Alexander Baird travelled to Bruges in Belgium in 1891 to watch his own fighter, Jem Smith, take on an Australian challenger, Frank Paddy Slavin ('the Sydney Cornstalk') in a barefisted contest which would by then have been illegal in Britain. It was instructive that Smith's opponent should have been Australian.

The antipodean penal colony had seen bareknuckle battles since its earliest days – in New South Wales on 8 January 1814, John Parton had defeated his fellow convict Charles Sefton after 90 minutes and 50 rounds. In 1847 the Englishman Isaac Read had defeated the Australian-born George Hough in Middle Head bushland after 98 minutes, in a fight which was never thought of as an international because Hough was, after all, simply an Englishman overseas. And in 1854 what was claimed to be the longest prize-fight ever recorded was slugged out over six hours at Fiery Creek between James Kelly and Jonathon Smith.

Smith and Kelly were reputed to have spent too much of the six hours in staring at each other and sparring in a desultory fashion. Australians were clearly ready for the Queensberry Rules, which duly arrived with the British champion Jem Mace in 1877. Mace, a former showman and circus performer, persuaded the Australian champion, Larry Foley, to put on gloves and box according to John Graham Chambers' legislation. Foley did so; but not until a prize-fighter named Alex Agar died in the Sydney ring in 1884 and his black American opponent was consequently jailed for a year did prize-fighting dip into decline in Australia.

So Frank Paddy Slavin, anxious to pursue his bareknuckle trade, was obliged to travel far from Sydney in 1891. He wound up facing Jem Smith in the Belgian back garden of a retired British army officer. And there he experienced the attentions of the last of the rakehells.

George Alexander Baird was dead at the age of 36, just two years after the affair at Bruges, and the fact surprised nobody. The heir to a Scottish coalmining fortune, he had been expelled from Eton twice, sent down from Cambridge University, and had eloped with the (married) Marquess of Aylesbury before reaching his majority. Having inherited, there was no stopping him.

He kept two stables, at Lickfield and Newmarket, which contained between them 250 thoroughbreds. Choosing often to ride his own mounts, he would diet on weak tea, castor oil and brandy, and once in the saddle George Baird knew no restraint: he scandalised even his fellows of the Fancy by trying to barge Lord Hartington and the favourite through the rails at Wolverhampton one day. By way of distraction, George Alexander Baird won the heart of Lily Langtry. According to popular legend, he introduced himself by presenting her with two betting slips to the value of £100, which they cashed and spent on one roistering night before winding up in bed.

Langtry may have been forewarned: Baird had already been sued by one woman for physical abuse. But she rode the storm for a year and more, until her servant woke her one afternoon to tell her that a riot was taking place at the Haymarket Theatre, where she was presently appearing. She made her way to the scene, and found that Baird and his friends had turned the foyer into a rat-pit. Terriers and large black rodents were engaged in a battle to the death, while the Fancy placed odds and yelled encouragement. Shortly afterwards a blow from Baird put Langtry in hospital, and she left this furious throwback for good; left him to put on cockfights in his own Newmarket mansion, and to match his bull-terrier 'Donald' against all-comers, and to hold huge banquets after which half the food was sticking to the walls, and to follow his bareknuckle champion, Jem Smith, to a back garden in Bruges to face Frank Paddy Slavin.

Smith got a hiding. By the 15th round Baird could no longer contain himself. Climbing drunkenly into the ring, he began to bellow: 'Do in the Australian bastard! Do in the Australian bastard!' He was forced out of the arena by his fellow member of the Pelican Club, Lord Mandeville, the heir to the Duchy of Manchester, who was obliged to draw a knife for the purpose.

Baird was subsequently ejected from the Pelican Club by its president and his exact contemporary at Eton, the Earl of Lonsdale. His time had gone. He sued at the Chancery Court to have his expulsion declared illegal, but failed, and in 1893 he travelled to America with the ageing fighter Charlie Mitchell in an expressed attempt to see Mitchell beat the world heavyweight champion Jim Corbett. The fight never took place. Baird went on a three-day drinking binge in New Orleans, and died.

His time had gone, but so had that of the Pelican Club. Shortly after the affair at Bruges it was dissolved and replaced by the National Sporting Club, which was also chaired by the Earl of Lonsdale. The National Sporting Club had nothing to do with bareknuckle prize-fights. It invited professional boxers to compete before its membership of merchants and aristocrats in after-dinner bouts staged according to the Queensberry Rules. Apart from seedy sideshows in Essex barns which persisted occasionally until the end of the twentieth century, boxing had found its respectable, modern, internationally recognised clothing.

'Fighting under the Marquis of Queensberry rules before gentlemen is a pleasure,' wrote the American champion John L. Sullivan in 1892, the year of his very first Queensberry Rules 'World

Title' fight against James J. 'Gentleman Jim' Corbett. Sullivan, who refused to fight black men on the grounds that to do so would diminish the dignity of the white race, was an advocate of the Queensberry Rules as much because they were respectable as because they were safe. As a fighter he was unique, partly because this American boxer became the world's first millionaire sportsman, but also because he spanned both eras. On 8 July 1889, just three years before his Queensberry contest with Corbett, he had defeated Jake Kilrain over two hours and 75 rounds in the 100-degree heat of a Mississippi summer, in what would become known as the last bareknuckle, Broughton's Code, American championship fight. When John L. Sullivan said that Queensberry Rules were best, people listened up.

His writ would finally run throughout the USA, but only after some hiccups. Occasionally the Americans displayed an alarmingly independent interpretation of John Graham Chambers' regulations. In 1893, for instance, Andy Bowen and Jack Burke proved in New Orleans that it was possible for gloved fighters to battle for longer than ungloved fighters, when they outdid the Australians of 1854 by boxing for seven hours 19 minutes, over 110 rounds, to a draw. In 1896 the state of New York ruled that boxing matches could legitimately continue for an indefinite number of rounds; and in 1911 the same state decided that fights of up to ten rounds could take place without a referee.

But it all settled down, and when it did, it became a pre-eminently American sport. The British invented the ring. The British gave boxing its first and most essential rules; they obviously provided the first 'world' champion, if Tom Cribb's half-forgotten fight with Tom Molineaux is to be registered; they joined the first boxing clubs; and they provided the first self-proclaimed international governing body in the form of the Amateur Boxing Asssociation, which was formed in 1881. But they lost control in the ring as soon as the early Americans adopted and properly adapted to the science of fighting which were catered to by the Queensberry Rules. And as they lost control in the ring, they lost control of the finances of the game. From the moments that first million-dollar gate was attracted to see Jack Dempsey fight Georges Carpentier in New Jersey in 1921, leading on to the 120,000 people crowded into the Sesqui-Centennial Stadium in Philadelphia five years later to see Dempsey versus Gene Tunney, the future of boxing was cast. It was American, and its currency was the dollar. It was a world which would not have been recognised by Jack Broughton, and which would have been raged against by George Alexander Baird, but it was a world which Baird's contemporary Hugh Cecil Lowther, the fifth Earl of Lonsdale, who lived until 1944, was to witness. By 1944 his Lonsdale Belts, which had first been issued to British champions in 1909, were as valued on the international boxing scene as a tiddlywinks trophy.

Boxing would continue to occupy a prominent place on Britain's imperial pantheon. Regarded always as one of the games which instilled the values of gentlemanly conquest, it would be offered up to youth after youth at public schools and other training camps ('Open order, march!' ran a famous British army order, 'Front rank, about turn! Box!'), but the products of those academies were never again any match for the hungry, streetwise fighters who issued from the Irish, the Italian, and ultimately the black ghettoes of the United States of America. The 'noble art' was lost to the British more conclusively than most others, and only in their nagging collective national memories could they pay homages to Jack Broughton, Tom Cribb, Jem Mace and the others. Still, it is curious and illuminating to note how many boxers of the eighteenth and nineteenth centuries are honoured with the company of the peers and merchants and military men who once sponsored them and employed them as bodyguards, within the august pages of the British *Dictionary of National Biography*.

The British found it difficult to relinquish their claim on the sports which they offered to the world (not least because in many of these early cases – before the high summer of imperial imperative – they had not actually offered them to the world: the world had come along and taken them uninvited), and the older the sport the more reluctant they were to cut the leading strings. In some cases this proprietorial vigour led a small, unfit and overstretched nation to quite unreasonable success both in administrative tenacity and playing accomplishment.

There have been sports more purely British in origin and in tone than golf. If British it is (and we choose to ignore the illustrations of seventeenth-century Hollanders swinging with clubs at small balls on the frozen canals, or the early records of Dutchmen playing a game called 'colf'), it is Scottish. Its Scottish origins will certainly derive from that northern Celtic branch of the bent-stick-and-ball game, camanachd. Records of the game of camanachd dating from the twelfth century AD indicate that it was frequently played by just one person, or by a pair, striking the ball towards a hole sunk into the ground, and etchings of golf from both Scotland and the Netherlands made in the seventeenth and eighteenth centuries show a golf club which has far more in common with a shinty stick than with a twentieth-century five-iron. Occasionally the terms were interchangeable: a shinty match would often commence with the ball being struck from a 'cogie', or crude golf tee, made from sand or earth piled into a small mound.

Certainly, in 1457 golf was included among the other games which were banned in Scotland by one of those dreary edicts which sought to protect archery practice. And in 1744 the Honourable Society of Edinburgh Golfers, the world's first golf club, which played on Leith Links, was established. Ten years later, in 1754, it was followed by the body which would become the internationally acknowledged alma mater and legislator of the game, the St Andrews Club, which would come to call itself the Royal and Ancient. (The struggle between the two Scottish originators was not finally resolved until 1895, when a Rules of Golf Committee was formed which consisted entirely of members of the Royal and Ancient.)

And for more than a century after 1754, golf would remain a Scottish pastime. Scottish exiles introduced it to Manchester and London in the early decades of the nineteenth century, but not until the 1860s were courses laid out for Englishmen (by Scots) in Devon and at Hoylake in Cheshire – and in 1879, when there were 72 golf clubs in the whole of Great Britain, no fewer than 52 of them were still in Scotland. It was so foreign south of the River Tweed that in 1830 an English visitor to Scotland felt obliged to describe the sport to his countrymen as if it were entirely unknown to them. 'The old Scots game of golf,' he wrote, 'is a gigantic variety of billiards; the table being a certain space in the green, sometimes of many hundreds of yards in extent – the holes situated here and there at great distances; and the balls, which are very hard, stuffed with feathers, being swung to and fro by means of long queues [cues] with elastic shafts – a fine healthful game.'

'Golf,' wrote the Englishman C.G. Heathcote of the game in England 60 years later, in 1890, 'the newest madness of recent years, was chartered by royalty and practised by a little band of worshippers for two centuries and a half before, in these last days, it claimed a home on every common, forced a club into every hand, and deposited a ball in every bunker.'

Golf was the great Scottish colonial export. The Scots began by infecting the English. Those 72 golf clubs throughout the UK in

1879 had become, by 1914, 2,844. The 20 English clubs of 1879 had become, 35 years later, 1,474 (not counting 17 in the Channel Islands and the Isle of Man). It was not an entirely ungrudging process: many Scots were fiercely jealous of their copyright on the sport and were reluctant to believe that it could, let alone should, be played elsewhere. 'Golf is attempted to be played in many places in England,' wrote a Scottish correspondent who dubbed himself 'Baffy' to the magazine *Golf* in 1895, 'about as fitted for the game as a summer fallow is for a game of cricket . . . We are all aware that one cannot make a silk purse out of a sow's ear or a proper golf links out of an old park, or fields of good inland pasture.'

But the momentum, once achieved, could not be denied. It is a plain but extraordinary fact that the first golf course to be laid outside Great Britain was constructed at Calcutta – by Scottish representatives of the Raj – as early as 1829, when there was barely a single purpose-built course in England. The links of the Royal Calcutta Golf Club were also among the lowest-lying in the world, their highest green standing just six feet above the River Ganges. 'Water,' the club's literature would admit, 'is a constant problem at every hole . . .' No such problems were encountered at Gulmarg in the Himalayas near Srinagar, where the Victorians built the highest golf course on earth at 8,700 feet above sea level.

To Scottish golfers, England was no more than another country which may or may not take up their game. In the 1820s the Scotsman Alexander Reid was playing golf with home-made clubs and a hand-fashioned feather-packed ball on his farm near Hobart, Tasmania. In Melbourne the Honourable James Graham was anxiously seeking partners, as was the solicitor John Dunsmore in Sydney, and as was the Governor of South Australia (and former Conservative MP for Ayrshire), Sir James Fergusson, in Adelaide between 1868 and 1873. In 1882 a crowd of native-born Australians gathered to watch the officers of a visiting Scottish regiment play an impromptu hole or two. When the soldiers had finished they gave their clubs and gutta-percha balls to the spectators, who then, according to legend, went off and formed the Australian Golf Club, the first of its kind in the antipodes. (The term 'gutta-percha', which commonly described the tightly bound late-Victorian golf ball which would be displaced at the end of the century by a rubber ball, was itself of imperial origin, coming from Malay words meaning 'gum' and 'strip of cloth'.) By 1894 the Australians had a national amateur golfing championship, a year after the New Zealanders had launched their own competition, and a year before the Canadians were to do the same – the Royal Montreal Golf Club had built itself a course in 1873.

The Americans are popularly supposed to have come late to golf. They did not. The same Scots who had taken their shinty sticks on to the frozen St Lawrence river were also playing golf in Charleston in 1786, and in Savannah in 1795. But no courses were built in the United States until 1887, when the Foxburg Golf Club, Pennsylvania, laid out its links. And after that neither golf nor the Americans looked back. They might have contented themselves with giving the game the term 'birdie', which was nineteenth-century US slang for 'excellent', but the American bourgeoisie chose instead to do for the Scottish game of golf what their working men had done for the English sport of boxing: they became its masters. Unlike boxing, they never chose to govern the game, that prerogative was left more or less safely in the hands of the Royal and Ancient at St Andrews, for which institution the American professional classes would develop a dewy-eyed, mystical regard. (When in 1958 President Dwight D. Eisenhower put up a new international golfing trophy to be called the Eisenhower Cup, its inaugural competition was played, at the request of the Americans, at St Andrews.) But on the greens they took control.

Golf being, like boxing, an individual exercise, it is certain that several accidental internationals took place between Scotsmen and Englishmen and Australians and Americans before, in 1902, the amateur golfers of England and Scotland met in the first official international contest. Scotland won by 32 holes to 25. The first amateur international between America and Britain took place at Hoylake in 1921. The Americans won comfortably, and they repeated the process in the following year when the series was played in Long Island for a piece of silverware known as the Walker Cup. And such was their domination of the biannual US versus Britain professional tournament which was played for the cup donated by Mr Samuel Ryder in 1927, that in 1977, with Great Britain having won only one of 16 tournaments since the end of the Second World War (and only three since 1927), it was agreed to replace the British select with one from the whole of the continent of Europe. The Spanish, Germans, Italians, French, Portuguese, Dutch and Belgians having all opened their own national golfing tournaments within five years of VE Day in 1945, as if it had been a stipulation of the Marshall Plan, this manoeuvre provided the Americans with stiffer opposition.

(1927, the year of the first Ryder Cup competition, was also, incidentally, the year when one Garnet Carter built a resort hotel called Fairyland on Lookout Mountain, Tennessee, and there devised a form of novelty golf for children which he called Tom Thumb Golf. This diversion would, when the adults had discovered their own fascination with it, sweep the world and make Garnet Carter's fortune as miniature golf. It was never a part of the grand international scheme of the Royal and Ancient Golf Club at St Andrews.)

Golf and boxing were hardly offered to the Americans in order that they might improve themselves; any more than it was anticipated by the British that their game would be so quickly improved upon by the audacious ex-colonials. The Scots and Englishmen who developed golf and boxing in the eighteenth and early nineteenth centuries were doing so for their pleasure alone. The same ferment of athletic creativity which led them to strike fixed codes for old and seemingly intransigent recreations, would bring virtually every sport known to the western world – or rather, those many of them which appealed to the British – under their firm administrative wing. Then, and only then, were they ready to proselytise their games.

They refined and they invented, and this very process – which came to be conducted with an almost manic energy – honed itself into an imperial mission. The most unusual of legislations occurred. The British modernisation of sport was a complex process. Just as several of their own early games, such as base ball and shinty on ice, were transported and adapted by the British overseas, so in many instances the old native sports of other lands which had been encountered on the imperial trail were adopted by the British abroad, brushed down, and offered back to the world (including their own countries of origin) in a presentable state. This fussy insistence on sporting codes and standards was precisely the same urge for order and civilised behaviour which led the Raj to hunt down Thuggee killers and to outlaw suttee, and which led them to erect lighthouses, build roads and sewers, and introduce Christianity to the pagan world. It merely took the British themselves longer to realise that their codified sports had a similar imperial dimension to religion and civic infrastructures.

The Field magazine of 3 August 1867 included the following report:

Captain Johnson brought over eighteen Iroquois Indians in the *Peruvian* last week, for the purpose of introducing the national game of Canada into England. The Iroquois tribe inhabit Lower Canada, near Montreal, and several of Captain Johnson's company were the same that performed the game before the Prince of Wales when in Canada in 1860. On Tuesday last a private performance took place at Beaufort House, Walham Green, under the patronage of Lord Ranelagh, at which members of the press and a few friends only were present. The Indians looked very smart, dressed in their blue and red drawers, the chiefs of each side being distinguished by feathers in their caps and other ornaments.

The game which these 18 Iroquois – who actually included among their number several half-breed Onondagas, Cayugas, Senecas, Oneidas, Mohawks and Algonquins – so dutifully performed before Lord Ranelagh at Beaufort House, was called by themselves baggataway, but was known to the Canadian British as lacrosse.

Baggataway had been a game of native North Americans, which legend suggested was first spotted in the eighteenth century by the French pioneer Charlevoix while he was ascending the St Lawrence river in Algonquin country. He named it not, as is popularly supposed, after a cross, but after the bishop's crozier which the game's curved stick brought to his mind. The French term for a crozier is 'crosse'. Curiously, this sport may not have originated with native Americans. 'Consider,' writes the linguist Bill Bryson, 'the matter of lacrosse, a game long popular with Indians across wide tracts of North America. Interestingly, the rules of lacrosse are uncannily like those of a game played by the Vikings, including one feature – the use of paired team-mates who may not be helped or impeded by other players – so unusual, in the words of one anthropologist, "as to make the probability of independent origin vanishingly small".'

By the eighteenth and nineteenth centuries those seafaring Scandinavians had forgotten all about this team game, however, and it had become purely the preserve of the Americans. Europeans were fascinated by lacrosse, not least because it took a form similar enough to be recognisable to anybody familiar with competitive sport in the Old World, while being at the same time markedly different to anything then played in Europe.

Their fascination had, on at least one occasion, bloody consequences. In the middle of the eighteenth century the British garrison at Detroit was so interested in lacrosse that its officers frequently invited the local Indians to play in the close environs of the fort. A chief named Pontiac, who had a predatory eye on the garrison, collected together one day a large party of Delawares, Ottawas and Shawanees, and commenced a game of lacrosse outside the Detroit stockade. At regular intervals the ball was accidentally struck into the fort, and a small group of Indians trotted inside to search for it. They did not return. Only after several such sorties were the garrison's suspicions aroused. The Indians within the compound were then driven back 'with great slaughter'.

In 1839 the Montreal Lacrosse Club, the first in the world (as native Americans did not draw up constitutions and codes), was established. In 1867 the British abroad formed the National La Crosse Association of Canada ('to improve, foster, and perpetuate the game of La Crosse as the national game of our dominion'), and wrote down a set of rules for a 12-a-side version of lacrosse, to be played between two goals measuring seven feet across by six high, on a pitch which was to be not more than 250 and not less than 150 yards long, and between 60 and 100 yards wide.

Those were the basic requirements of Victorian team games: a prescribed size of field and goal, and a limited number of persons per team. They were the essential first steps for every codified sport, and the main striking difference between team games as visualised by the organising British, and their hectic, unlegislated forerunners, which had without exception been played by as many as wished to take part, on a strip of land which knew no real boundaries other than those dictated by the laws of trespass, or the village boundaries which in some games served as the goal-lines.

In the same year, 1867, Captain Johnson's colourful touring party of 18 Indians visited England, and the first British club was established in Glasgow. The following year, 1868, saw the formation of the English Lacrosse Association, as well as the introduction of the organised game to the United States through the Mohawk Club of Troy, New York.

But by 1868 the British at home were not content simply to import sports, even those sports which had been codified in the dominions by the British abroad. Just as we have seen that they could not, well into the twentieth century, relinquish the reins of bowling, so by the seventh decade of the nineteenth century the British had become more or less convinced that they, back home in Britain, knew best. Anything issuing from overseas would be by definition flawed.

So when, in 1868, the English Lacrosse Association published its own rules of the game, which differed only slightly from those published a year earlier by the Canadian body, there was little doubt at home which rules were preferable. Despite the fact that the sport of lacrosse had been played in America since (possibly) the time of the Vikings a millennium earlier (and equally possibly, for even longer), and had only been seen for the first time in Britain just 12 months before, the rules drawn up in England were deemed, in England, to be unarguably the better.

It was imperial arrogance, of course. And it was beautifully articulated. 'One or more sets of Canadian [lacrosse] rules,' pronounced a guide to outdoor games which was published in England in that same year, 1868, 'have been sold in this country, but they have been unanimously abandoned by the clubs in favour of the [English] Association rules here given.

'It cannot be doubted that these rules are greatly superior to the Canadian, and that they are the best which English experience has yet been able to devise.'

This matter of English experience was a wonderful thing. By 1868 it was truly marvellous that there should be a single recreation extant anywhere in the world, which had not been invented between Land's End and Berwick – or, to allow a point, between Land's End and John O'Groats.

'It seems strange,' mused that 1868 guide to outdoor sports, 'that England should sit at the feet of the foreigner for instruction in manly sports. The ancient home of cricket, football, and a host of minor games – the natural abode of all sport – she is accustomed to teach rather than to learn. Has not 'le sport' become a French phrase, in the utter absence of a native word for such a purely English notion?'

The next two sentences were written as they were intended to be read: perfectly straight-faced, with an absolute absence of irony. As an expression of the high Victorian attitude towards Britain, non-Britain, and sport, they were never bettered: 'And can any good thing come out of foreign parts?' wondered that 1868 sporting guide. 'In matters of sport is not the world divided into two parties? – the one Greeks, the other barbarians; we being the Greeks, and all other nations whatsoever the barbarians.'

These latterday Greeks, so confident of their superiority, could nonetheless accommodate the occasional import. It was a sign of their easy magnanimity. Our guide to sport in 1868 assured his readers:

There seems a good prospect of a beautiful foreign game becoming thoroughly at home among us. Like other importations, La Crosse, the illustrious stranger, has more grace and elegance about it than similar articles of home manufacture. There is nothing very graceful in football, thoroughly English game though it be. A 'maul', with half a dozen Britons kicking each other's shins, is perhaps amusing as a spectacle, and is certainly evidence of national pluck and good temper, but a foreigner may be excused for holding it in some contempt. Then again, too many of our games are dangerous.

Certainly we have no maudlin horror of a spice of danger, for we remember that those who led the six hundred over Russian guns at Balaclava had learnt the trick from five-barred gates at home. We even think that square-leg to a hard hitter is no bad training for coolness at the 'cannon's mouth'. But while many bold spirits will always love the rough games for their roughness, many will welcome a safe game . . .

In short, no foreigner could be expected to adapt to the unique robustness and characteristic bravery of rugby or cricket. Nobody from abroad, perhaps not even the British abroad, could possibly appreciate the imperial bullishness which formed those who entered a rugger scrum, or who fielded at square-leg to a slogger. The British themselves, on the other hand, were superhumanly capable both of hacking away at shins and of enjoying the softer virtues of such non-British games as lacrosse.

They were also divinely qualified to adjust the poor foreigners' clumsy attempts at legislation. If the British did not do so, who would? Had not the British – and not the British abroad – invented the very process of codifying sports? 'The Canadian rules,' explained our 1868 authority on lacrosse, 'are much more minute than ours, and seek to provide laws for all sorts of matters which we in England prefer to leave to honourable understanding amongst the players . . .

'The colonists have not been schooled in the continual playing of games where written laws are unknown, so they pile up safeguards as if the combatants were going to law instead of playing a match.'

There is an unsubtle shift of attitude to be spotted here, from the Georgian days when it was simply considered that nobody overseas could play games except the colonial British, and that even they did so comparatively poorly. The colonists and their subject peoples were by the second half of the nineteenth century allowed a degree of ability at some sports (although only a degree: it was considered that the year 1868, after lacrosse had been played in England for just 12 months, was too early to consider challenging the Canadians in an international fixture, 'but in 1869 surely some of our clubs will be proficient enough to give a worthy reception to the travellers from the New Dominion'). But the colonists from the dominions were not to be trusted with either legislation or authority. That was the preserve of the British in Britain.

If they could get away with governing the old native American game of lacrosse, they could get away with anything. And they did. The first international lacrosse fixture was not, in the end, between Canada and England. It occurred in 1875, and it featured England and Scotland (Scotland won 4–3). Not until 1883 did a Canadian lacrosse team visit the United Kingdom, when the men from the 'New Dominion' defeated a combined Great Britain select side by 12–1. They were followed in 1888 by the Toronto Lacrosse Club, which won its six consecutive matches on British soil, scoring 54 goals and conceding just 13.

And yet, when it came to legislating for the international sport of lacrosse, the game's originators and dominant competitors were left entirely without office. In 1892 the North of England and South of England Lacrosse Associations, which had been running regional 'Flag Competitions' since 1884, amalgamated into the English Lacrosse Union. This body replaced the old English Lacrosse Association, and one of its self-ordained functions was to 'control international lacrosse matters'. The Canadians were, after all, citizens of a dominion of Great Britain, and their dominion status applied as much to sport as it did to matters of taxation and conscription. Once assumed, the mantle of responsibility was not easily to be removed. Typically, the idiosyncratics of the United States would occasionally insist upon a degree of independence, as when in 1933 they insisted upon reducing the number of players per side in their own excellent lacrosse teams to ten. But as late as 1958, when the laws of international lacrosse were entirely redrawn, the body which undertook the task was the English Lacrosse Union.

If not the British, then who? Nobody else was interested, it seemed, in organising games – not even their own games. The Victorians, convinced by the 1860s and 1870s of their own heavenly mission to put the world into parade-ground order, could and did look around the scarlet-speckled globe and ask themselves, what chaos would otherwise be found?

'Polo,' writes the sports historian Richard D. Mandell, 'or comparable competitive displays of strenuous horsemanship were (and in many places still are) common from Hungary to Manchuria and from Arabia to the Caucasus . . . there still exist ancient polo fields in Isfahan and Shiraz and in other great cities of central Asia.'

The British imperial cavalry in India were fascinated by polo, as the British trappers and tradesmen in Canada had been by lacrosse. They appear first to have encountered this essentially Persian sport in north-east India, where it was played by the local aristocracy, and they took to it wonderfully. By the 1850s British planters and soldiers were playing matches against Indian opposition. This led inevitably to the formation of a club, and in 1859 the Silchar Polo Club was established by Europeans in India. It was followed hotly by the Calcutta Polo Club in 1862, and according to regimental legend it was that most fashionable of all the cavalry troops of the Raj, the 9th Queen's Royal Lancers, who first played polo, or 'hockey on horse-back' as they dubbed it, in England, at Hounslow Heath in 1871. An observer apparently thought their display to be 'more remarkable for the strength of the language used by the players than for anything else'.

Polo became an integral part of the officer-class imperial experience. 'As a soldier,' wrote the 21-year-old Second Lieutenant Winston Spencer Churchill to his mother from Bangalore in 1896, 'my intelligent interests are supposed to stop short at polo, racing & Orderly Officer.' Churchill was, in fact, like so many of his class and generation, devoted to the game – he played it throughout his time in India, and did not perform in his last chukka until 1926, when he found himself at a loose end in the colonial property of Malta, at the age of 52 years. At 5 p.m. at his posting in India, he would later recall with affection, 'The station begins to live again. It is the hour of Polo. It is the hour for which we have been living all day long.' And he remembered that: 'Tournaments in Hyderabad were a striking spectacle. The whole ground was packed with enormous masses of Indian spectators of all classes, watching the game with keen and instructed attention. The tents and canopies were thronged with the British community and the Indian rank and fashion of the Deccan.'

Native peoples appear frequently to have exploited this strange British obsession with their recreations. Just as Pontiac had attempted to use a display of lacrosse to bamboozle the Detroit garrison a century earlier, so in 1895 Major George Robertson, a political officer in the British Army of India, was almost undone by a quaint piece of polo treachery. Robertson had set out in the spring of that year with 400 troops to overthrow the ruler of a remote and troublesome central Himalayan Emirate at Chitral. Having done so he sat tight and awaited reinforcements and a fresh supply of ammunition.

These, in the shape of two British subalterns and a Kashmiri troop, were on their way through the mountains when they were ambushed by Chitralis and were obliged to seek safety in a small village. The Chitralis at first laid siege, and then appeared to relent and negotiated a cease-fire. They supplied the invaders with food and water, and suggested that the newfound accord should be celebrated by a display of polo on open ground before the British positions. The two subalterns were invited to watch as guests of honour. Having little choice, they did just that, covered by their Kashmiri marksmen. The Chitralis played polo, and then began – as was their custom – to dance, insinuating themselves between the subalterns and their men. The British officers, who had presumably been made relaxed and careless by the whole sporting display, were seized, bound, and dragged away, and the Kashmiris were slaughtered. Robertson was eventually relieved by another force, but the subalterns were never seen again.

The Chitralis, like Pontiac's Delawares, had identified an obsessive weakness. The conquering British could not leave games alone. Presented with an athletic contest they dropped everything to watch or to participate. But what the Himalayans and the American Indians perceived as folly, the British were doggedly transforming in their own minds into an international asset.

They took the game of polo, as eastern a pursuit as lacrosse had been North American, and they carried it with them back to Europe, recreating it in their own image. The wild and violent, semi-regulated equestrian contest of old Isfahan and Shiraz was, in 1874, delivered into the steady, rational hands of a committee of the newly formed Hurlingham Polo Association. Its teams were limited by these gentlemen to four-a-side; its pitch was prescribed at 300 by 160 yards; its goals were determined to be 24 yards wide; and after that, as the 'Badminton Library' annual put it: 'Many regiments took up the game; the Universities did the same . . . polo was becoming a popular amusement; the International Gun and Polo Club started operations at Brighton, and soon all chance of the game falling into obscurity was provided against.'

And, of course, just as these newly standardised regulations both appealed to the British at home and enabled the universities and the regiments to play meaningful matches against each other, so those same rules facilitated the sport's spread abroad. Don Pedro Gonzales Soto, who would become the Marquis de Torre-Soto, first encountered polo while visiting friends in Kent. Once back in Spain he sought out three British residents there, Richard Davies, John Foster and Roderick Crewell, and the four men established in 1874 the Jerez Polo Club, the first polo club outside India or England, which is to say, the first which was not on British soil.

Two years later, in 1876, the game reached the New World when Mr James Gordon-Bennett established the Westchester Polo Club at Newport. Predictably, almost uniquely in the civilised sporting world, the Americans would shortly defy the right of the British in Britain to dictate the codes and discipline of international sport. In 1891 the United States Polo Association (which was at the time an impertinent one-year-old) decided that, contrary to Hurlingham regulations, individual players should be handicapped. They did not carry the whole of the United States with them – five Californian polo clubs which had been started by Englishmen promptly declared that as San Francisco was farther from New York than New York was from London, they would play by Hurlingham rules. The Americans did, however, eventually succeed in eliciting an unusual degree of flexibility from a British governing body: in 1910 their handicapping system was accepted in both England and India.

And so it spread: to Deauville and Paris and Cannes (where Winston Churchill was, in Edwardian times, an occasional com-petitor); to Melbourne in the 1870s; to New Zealand and South Africa in the 1880s; and most crucially to the future development of the international game, to Argentina where, in 1885, English ranchers discovered a new and exciting way of exercising their many horses and of displaying their excellent horsemanship, and where in 1892 the River (not Rio) Plate Polo Association was formed, and where at the beginning of the twentieth century what would become the largest such body in South America was christened, in unapologetic tribute, the Hurlingham Polo Club of Buenos Aires.

British hegemony over international sport was, by the fourth quarter of the nineteenth century, almost complete. What few globally recognised games they had not invented, they had adopted and transformed and, subsequently, governed. Most remarkably, perhaps, was the fact that there seemed to be no limit to the British taste. Any sport, large or small, would do . . .

CHAPTER SIX

Anyone for Tennis?

Playing a ball over a net by striking it with a racket, which is the main feature of Lawn Tennis, is one of the best ways of getting a great deal of exercise in a short time.

A limitation of Lawn Tennis, however, is that the Court requires a lot of space, and for that reason it is mainly an open-air, fair-weather game. Table Tennis is a sort of miniature Lawn Tennis which is played indoors; it cannot take the place of Lawn Tennis, however, as it does not provide as much exercise.

If you stop to think for a moment, you will see that the space required for a Lawn Tennis Court could be halved if, instead of hitting the ball over a net it could be played against a wall so that it would bounce back into play . . .

The Boy's Book of Sport, Carlton Wallace, 1951

The variety was extraordinary. Throughout the nineteenth century sports were organised in and flung out of Great Britain like confetti. The establishment of the club, the embracing of the notion of sport as a social activity around which people throughout the burgeoning Empire (and, if they saw fit, those outside it) could organise their leisure hours, left no recreation untouched. And as the club had led directly to the constitution and codes of play, all of the affected pursuits became potentially international in their scope.

The result would ultimately be a sterilisation of sport, because once the Victorians had finished their work the world would be equipped with a broad repertoire of games whose rules were set in soft stone. Individual communities would no longer feel the need to develop their own idiosyncratic games, or their own idiosyncratic versions of established games. The development of wholly new recreations in the twentieth century was seen as broadly unnecessary, and hardly ever occurred (although many of the established pursuits were further refined), and those old games which had slipped through the net were largely lost for ever to a thoughtless world. But to the Victorians, that was all in the unimaginable future: while their organisational process was under way it was vibrant and exciting and astonishingly creative. The most unlikely games intermarried and bred with great fertility. There seemed no reason, at the time, for any deserving sport to miss the boat.

Shortly after his incarceration in London's Fleet Prison, Samuel Weller, the hero of Charles Dickens's *Pickwick Papers*, repaired to the prison's skittle ground with a refreshing pint of porter purchased from the prison tap, and sat down upon a bench with a two-day-old newspaper. 'Then he read two lines of the paper, and stopped short to look at a couple of men who were finishing a game at rackets, which, being concluded, he cried out "wery good" in an approving manner, and looked round upon the spectators, to ascertain whether their sentiments coincided with his own.'

Dickens wrote the *Posthumous Papers of the Pickwick Club* in 1836 and 1837. Rackets was a variant of one of the older European pastimes: there were records of such a game, which involved hitting a ball against a wall with such force or subtlety that its rebound evaded one's opponent, being played by medieval French monks who used not a racquet, but their bound clenched fists, and who therefore christened the game 'cinque', or fives. (When the flat palm of the hand was used it was known, equally predictably, as 'jeu de paume'.) The pupils of Eton and Rugby schools came to play their own versions of cinque, which were known as Eton Fives and Rugby Fives, the chief – if not the only – differences between the two being that Eton Fives was purely a doubles game, whereas Rugby Fives permitted singles contests, and the wall of an Eton Fives court was distinguished by having a buttress (known as a 'pepper') jutting out from one side. (The game would spread in the later nineteenth century to a number of lesser public schools. The diabolist Aleister Crowley, who was educated at Malvern in the 1890s, introduced a little touch of home to his monastery at Cefalu in Sicily in the 1920s by using its backyard as a fives court.) Elsewhere, by the seventeenth century the boys of Harrow School had seized upon another variant of the game, and were using crude racquets to hit a ball against a wall in a yard of the old school building. This was a loud activity: *racquet* was French for 'noise'; its anglicisation, 'racket', would come of course to mean both the hubbub and the game and its instrument. By 1830 those Harrovians appear to have discovered that when a punctured ball hit the wall, it squashed upon impact. This limited bounce obviously made for a sport which could be contained within a small area, such as the skittles yard of the Fleet Prison, and it also produced a greater variety of rebound, which in turn demanded a keener response from the players. Harrow School celebrated its invention by building, in 1850, two uncovered rackets courts, one of which had only one side wall.

Those were the origins of fives, rackets, squash and hardball. The differences between the three remains chiefly that fives, or handball, does not require a racquet; while of the two games which do, squash – which was originally known as squash rackets, and did not officially abbreviate its name until 1992 – is played upon a smaller court and originally with a softer ball than rackets; and that hardball is squash played – most often in America in the first half of the twentieth century – not with a soft but a hard ball.

The differences, in other words, always have been negligible. But it was as four distinct and proudly independent sports that British men, chiefly of the soldiery, took with them around the world. The officers of Canadian military garrisons at Montreal, Hamilton, Quebec and Halifax, doubtless inspired by recollections of their school-days, were all playing rackets at the close of the eighteenth century, and there appears to have been a rackets club in Montreal by 1800, although proof positive of its existence did not materialise until 1825.

By the close of the first half of the nineteenth century a Canadian named Edward H. La Montagne had introduced the game of rackets to the United States, and courts were built firstly in New York's Bowery district, and then at the premises of the Broadway Racquet Club (the Americans, ornery as ever, insisted always upon the original French spelling of the word for 'noise'). A delightful description remains of the balls used in such contests: they were 'of a very fine quality, made of white woollen yarn, dampened and wound tightly around a piece of solid rubber about the size of a marble. They were covered with white kid and sewed with silk of various colours: blue, yellow and scarlet. A box of balls was a pretty sight.'

By the end of the nineteenth century there were 70 rackets courts across the Indian subcontinent from Rangoon to Bombay. A Parsee professional, a marker at the Bombay Gymkhana named Jamsetji, visited London in 1903 and there beat Gilbert Browne 5–1 to

become the first non-Briton to win the World Rackets Championship, which had been played for intermittently since 1820. (The word
'gymkhana' entered the English language from the Hindustani *gend-
khana*, or ball-house, which was what the Indians called a rackets and
squash court.) Jamsetji was quickly followed by the great Jock Soutar
of the Philadelphia Racquet Club, who won the title on three consecutive attempts in 1914, 1923 and 1927, before eventually
succumbing to his old rival Charles Williams of Chicago in 1928.

But slowly and steadily, across North America and the properties
of the Raj, rackets courts were transformed into the smaller squash
courts so that more men could play at any given time. James P.
Conover, the headmaster of St Paul's School in Concord, New
Hampshire, first saw squash (as opposed to rackets) being played in
Montreal during a visit to Canada in the early 1880s, and he decided
that it would be a good game for his boys, provided that they enjoyed
'but one rubber a day . . . for health and for highest perfection'. So
Mr Conover returned to Concord and set about building the first
squash rackets court in the United States of America. Before doing
so, he explained in his school magazine that the game had its
substantial advantages, despite being less fast and exciting and
dangerous ('enticing' was the word he used) than the big old sport of
racquets. The headmaster wrote in 1882:

> The building will cover an area of fifty feet by sixty and will have
> a height of about seventy feet from the ground to the eaves, and
> will be covered with a plain peaked roof.
>
> The ball used in such courts is about the size of a walnut, of
> rubber, and hollow, with a hole in it to prevent breaking. In such
> a court, the game is not quite so enticing as where the walls are
> of brick and the ball solid, like a small base-ball. But the so-called
> 'squash-ball court' recommended itself to the club for many
> reasons: such courts are largely used in English public schools:
> cost of construction is much less: fewer racquet bats are broken
> and fewer balls destroyed: fewer heads are cracked and fewer
> knees and elbows barked: the danger from being hit by the ball
> (quite an item among young players) is cancelled: and for all
> intents and purposes the game is the same and produces just as
> good players.

Squash was slow to supplant rackets as the privileged man's game
in both of its future heartlands: the United States of America and the

imperial dominions of Great Britain. The older game of rackets, which was perceived as being more heroic, continued to monopolise the affections of colonial governors and soldiers until well into the twentieth century – indeed, it was not until 1923 that H.A.L. Rudd, writing in *Baily's Magazine*, greeted the first English Amateur Squash Championships with the prediction that rackets would lose many players to squash, a prospect which Rudd regarded with gloom, as rackets in his opinion was both manlier and more skilful.

But Rudd was right. The advantages of squash which the New Hampshire headmaster James Conover had enumerated in 1882, and which his fellow Americans had been quick to explore, proved to be seductive. The game demanded much less space and at least an equal portion of skill, while being rather less furious than rackets.

The precise dimensional differences between squash and rackets were first defined by the Bath Club in London, where a court was built at the turn of the nineteenth century into the twentieth. This court measured 32 feet by 21 feet, whereas a rackets court was 60 feet by 30 feet. But once that was done (and the sizes were internationally ratified in 1923) America, with its hardball game, and the dominions, with their softball game, pointed the way. The first club to be devoted by the Britons abroad purely to squash rackets was formed in Toronto in 1908. The first national squash championships outside the USA (which had formed a United States Squash Rackets Association in 1907 and staged its first tournament in that year) was played in South Africa in 1910. In 1913 the Melbourne Rackets Club converted its one rackets court into two squash courts. The earlier imperialists, those who had moved with seamless grace from Harrow to Oxford to Delhi or the Sudan, had cared little for the use of an excess of space (there was after all, as the British rapidly found out, a lot of unclaimed space in the world). But the commissioned officers of a later date were both thicker on the ground and usually more impecunious, and squash, to them, made better sense.

In two particular countries this conversion had a remarkable effect. In the territories of northern India which would become, after independence and partition, Pakistan, and in Egypt during the British Protectorate of late-Victorian and Edwardian times, the occupying British military built a substantial number of rackets courts. They employed at those institutions many local boys as markers and court cleaners. When the rackets courts were converted into squash courts, and as, in the dying years of the Protectorate and of the Raj, the colonial societies became marginally more open, several of those local men took to playing the game that they had devoted a young working life to studying.

They became in short, stunning order the best in the world. In 1933 the Egyptian F.D. Amr Bey travelled to London to take part in the British Open Squash Championships. These were widely regarded as the World Championships. That was not because they could claim any great antiquity: the British had been organising squash tournaments only since 1922, and not until 1928 did they even have an independent Squash Rackets Association, which had wrenched itself free from the Tennis and Rackets Association. It was only because the British catered for softball squash, which was played throughout all of the world other than the USA, Canada and Mexico, whose national tournaments used hardballs on slightly smaller courts.

So to non-American squash players London was the only arena which could cater for the world which London had once dominated, and it was to London that F.D. Amr Bey journeyed in 1933. He won the British Open that year, and he won it a further four times between 1934 and 1937. And when Amr Bey, who had learned the game of squash at a British military club in Cairo, had stopped winning the international championships of what we might call the pre-war British world, his countryman Mahmoud Karim took over and monopolised the post-war British Open Squash Championships between 1947 and 1950. Karim had no sooner hung up his racquet than an extraordinary dynasty from another former district of the Empire, one which had inherited as many old British military squash courts as had Egypt, stepped forward. Hashim Khan of Pakistan eclipsed both Karim and Amr Bey by winning the British title each year between 1951 and 1956. His cousin Roshan Khan won it in 1957; Hashim took it back in 1958; Azam Khan then took over between 1959 and 1962; and Hashim's nephew Mohibullah Khan held the trophy in 1963. These wonderfully gifted men, who were born as imperial subjects, took care to stress their international superiority by also winning the North American Squash Championships: Hashim and Roshan on three occasions each; Azam once; and Mohibullah four times.

There was then a hiatus, during which the titles were dominated by Ireland's Jonah Barrington and Australia's Geoff Hunt. (Ireland, with its fair share of British barracks, had been offered the game as early in the century as had Egypt and Pakistan; Australia, which by the first decade of the twentieth century was no longer a nation policed by military might, came to it rather later.) But in 1982 a new generation of Khans, spearheaded by Jahangir and Jansher, commenced a fresh decade of Pakistani ascendency. In the whole of this period since Amr Bey's first victory in 1933 there was no British squash player who came remotely close to equalling the achievements of Amr Bey, Karim, the Khans, Barrington or Hunt. And yet when in 1966 it was agreed to merge the two bodies with claims on the international governance of the sport, the Squash Rackets Association of England and the United States Squash Racquets Association, all of the major competing nations travelled to found the International Squash Rackets Association in the capital of the old empire, London. And by the end of the twentieth century the game, whose original form Sam Weller had applauded on the skittles ground of the Fleet Prison, was being played on 46,000 courts in 122 countries by over 15 million men and women around the world. 'Wery good,' he cried out in an approving manner . . .

Racquet and ball games delighted the Anglo-Saxons: they contained so much scope for variety. As late as 1950 a man called Joe Sobek was inventing yet another alternative to squash racquets in the gymnasium of Greenwich Young Men's Christian Association in Connecticut, USA. He called it racquetball, and its essential differences to the parent games were that the ball was larger and the racquets had shorter handles. It was, in fact, something of a reversion to *jeu de paume*.

Sobek was continuing in an honourable tradition. For centuries British children had played an old racquet and ball game called battledore and shuttlecock. This pursuit demanded co-operation rather than competition, in that its object was for two people to bat the feathered shuttlecock between each other, keeping it in the air for as long as possible, much as the late twentieth-century French, disinterested in scoring points while on vacation, would develop a beach game which involved keeping a small rubber ball airborne with the help of table tennis bats.

Battledore and shuttlecock became, in the first half of the nineteenth century, a popular outdoor recreation for the British in the still, open air of the tropics. Its non-competitive ethos would not, however, satisfy the Victorians for long . . .

The legend, which will serve as an educative parable of the birth of such sports if not as an account of precise historical fact, has it that in or around the year 1860 two young daughters of the Duke of Beaufort were playing battledore and shuttlecock in the great hall of Badminton House, the Gloucestershire seat of the Somerset family.

In order to increase the degree of difficulty, the girls rigged up a string between a doorhandle and the fireplace and agreed that the shuttlecock must be driven over the string.

Thereafter the mists of mythology grow even thicker. A group of houseguests emerge from them. Occasionally they are Indian Army officers on furlough; occasionally they include J.L. Baldwin, a popular and inventive sportsman who is known to have been a frequent visitor to Badminton House. One of these ghostly characters suggested to the little Somersets that it might be amusing if, instead of directing the shuttlecock so that the other player could return it with ease, the thing should be struck with sufficient force and accuracy to evade the girl on the other side of the string.

Badminton returned to India as a competitive sport. Its first rules were prepared at Poona in 1875 by Colonel H.O. Selby, with the result that the game was known for several decades in the subcontinent not as badminton, but as poona. The British at home were not slow, however, in reasserting their claim. By the late 1870s and 1880s retired army officers and their wives were gaily knocking home-made shuttlecocks over nets on large hourglass-shaped courts in groups of four or five a side in the genteel suburbs of London and in such places of retirement as Folkestone, Teignmouth, Bognor Regis, Portsmouth, Bath and Southsea. In 1887 J.H.E. Hart adapted Colonel Selby's Poona rules to the specific indoor requirements of Bath Badminton Club, and in 1893 the English Badminton Association was established under the avuncular chairmanship of Colonel S.M.C. Dolby.

The game was slow to seed. Only a dozen clubs united to form the EBA in 1893, and five years later it had just 20 affiliated bodies. But by 1901 the number had risen to 65, and by that date badminton had also been introduced to Dublin, to New York (whose badminton club boasted of being the oldest in the world), to Auckland, New Zealand, and to the Army Drill Hall at Fremantle, Western Australia. In 1899 the first All-England Badminton Championships were held in London, and in 1903 the first international badminton match was played between England and Ireland.

The International Badminton Federation was convened in 1934 by the English association in collaboration with its colleagues from the white dominions. One country was, most notably as it turned out, at first excluded. Malaya had only just formed its own Badminton Association in 1934, but it would not stage the first All-Malayan Championships until 1937.

It was not so very far for a game to travel, in the late-Victorian and Edwardian decades, between Gloucestershire and Singapore. Badminton was taken to Malaysia not — as was most common elsewhere — by the military, but by Anglican and Methodist missionaries. The game which had been invented by the Duke of Beaufort's two little daughters was seen by these evangelists as a useful and decorous means of exercising the minds and bodies of the Asian young. Such formidable women as Josephine Foss, an Anglican missionary firstly to China and then to Pudu in Malaya in 1925, were convinced that Malaysian boys and girls alike required healthy physical exercise as an alternative to the lures of prostitution, the opium dens and gambling. People such as Ms Foss were educational progressives. Foss herself had been pained by the sight of girls' bound feet in China, and was determined that her young female charges should, rather than suffering under such a yoke because of reactionary tradition, be set free to develop their bodies as naturally as any British or American child. Josephine Foss was also a keen badminton player.

In this sense, badminton became one of the games which the British (and some of Josephine Foss's American allies) deliberately introduced to colonised peoples in order to improve their spirit and physique. Not all sports followed that path, as we have seen and as we will see, but several did, and for many different reasons. Badminton was not delivered to Malaysian children because it was considered that the game itself had any intrinsic moral or spiritual virtues which were not possessed by other sports. Indeed, gymnastics, callisthenics, athletics, cycling, swimming, cricket, hockey, soccer, tennis, volleyball, netball, basketball and — of all things — quoits, were all deployed by the missionaries in Malaya and in much of the rest of south-east Asia. In the view of the Anglicans and Methodists, the game of badminton possessed none of the mystique which, say, cricket had for imperialists of another school; and it had none of the character-developing qualities of a rugby scrimmage.

To those men and women of the travelling church, sport itself was the saviour, as a wholesome Christian alternative to a dire upbringing in a traditional Malaysian society — sport itself, almost any sport, could help to liberate the youngsters from the bound limbs and bound minds of their elders, and assist them towards seeing the world through western eyes. Physical education, wrote Mrs W.E. Curtis of the Methodist Teacher Girls' School in Taiping in 1901, had become 'one of the most profitable features of the school.

'It has not only benefited the children mentally and physically but has elicited the interest of persons who have given financial and other aid to the school. We have held a monthly gymnastic competition for which prizes have been kindly presented by ladies of Taipeng.'

Show me, insisted the Methodist Mabel Marsh – who believed that the Chinese gambled so much because 'they have never had the play instinct developed and do not know a better way of spending their leisure time' – 'Show me a girl who does not enjoy such games and I will show you a girl whose home environment has inhibited all her desire for self-expression, or else one who is physically unfit to play.'

Badminton took to Malaya, and the Malayans took to badminton, not because it was necessarily the preferred recreation of all the colonial missionaries to the country, but because the Malayans themselves turned out to be very, very good at it.

Just how good the rest of the world would not discover until after the Second World War. By that time quite a number of international matches had been played between the white dominions and the first European country to adopt the game, Denmark. In 1948 an international badminton championship was launched for the Thomas Cup. It was launched with confidence by the English, who had never lost a single international team match since their first defeat of Ireland by 5–2 in Dublin in 1903. Eleven nations competed in three zones. The United States won the American Zone, Denmark beat England 9–0 in Copenhagen to win the European Zone . . . and Malaya had a walkover through lack of competition in the Pacific Zone.

Those three teams then assembled in Great Britain to play off for the Thomas Cup. The results were sensational. Malaya, who had never previously met any other country in an international fixture of any kind, beat firstly the United States 6–3 in Glasgow, and then travelled to Preston to dismiss Denmark 8–1. Rashly, the English were not convinced of the true quality of the players from their former colony, and they invited the Malayans to Torquay in 1949 for a friendly international. Malaya won it 9–0. Wong Peng Soon, Ooi Teik Hock, Ong Poh Lim and the Choong brothers then proceeded to dominate not only the Thomas Cup, but also the All-England Championships for the next ten years, until they were finally defeated in Singapore in 1958 by Thailand. Not all of the missionary work of Anglicans and Methodists in south-east Asia would have such dramatic or lasting effect.

Among the tempting sports and recreations which were dangled like a mobile before the eager young eyes of the children of Malaya was a Victorian parlour game called ping-pong. This apparently harmless diversion suffered a controversial early life. Rarely can any game have been so riven by debate over its name.

The mid-Victorians called it ping-pong in imitation of the sound made by a small cork ball striking a cleared dining table and a vellum bat. Ping-pong was, however, quickly seized upon and marketed by various entrepreneurs. The sports equipment manufacturers Jaques & Co decided, for reasons which are unclear, that the name of the game should be 'gossima'. Another supplier christened it 'whiff-whaff'. By the end of 1901 a group of true sportsmen had decided to form the Table Tennis Association 'to keep the control in the hands of amateur players themselves, and independent of trade influence'.

They were not wholly successful, and their association was shortlived. In 1902 there were no fewer than 49 different types of bat on the market, and in the same year young Master John Jaques III, having inherited his family concern, relaunched the game in boxed sets. He dropped the name 'gossima', and registered 'ping-pong' as a trademark. The Ping-Pong Association was founded that year to promote Jaques & Co's product. It caused some ill-feeling. Jaques' boxed sets of ping-pong equipment were illustrated by gentlemen and ladies playing the game while wearing full Edwardian evening dress, but an article published in 1903 felt it necessary to warn enthusiasts that dress suits, stiff shirts and white satin gowns were not the recommended apparel for a game of whatever it might be called. The furore finally came to a head in 1921 when the Ping-Pong Association, which had died in 1905, was revived as an independent body. Its executive quickly discovered that the term ping-pong was still a registered trademark (it was by then in the hands of Parker Brothers Ltd, the games people) and they equally quickly changed their own name to the Table Tennis Association, just in time for the first English Open Table Tennis Championships in 1922.

It had, in the meantime, attracted the attention of one Professor Seizo Tsuboi who, after a visit to London in the early years of the century, packed up a paddle and a ball and took them back with him to Tokyo. And for reasons which are equally inscrutable the game had also – while the English were arguing their invention to death – been happily welcomed in Austria, Romania, Hungary and Czechoslovakia.

Table tennis would never become a particularly popular game in either the old or the new dominions. It was effectively ignored by the Americans, and even in Australia, whose white population could normally be depended upon to ape all aspects of recreational fashion in the old country, and where the game of ping-pong was being played at Adelaide as early as 1898. It was not until the 1930s that a small organisational body was formed.

But in central Europe and in the Asian countries of Japan and – thereafter – the Japanese areas of influence in China and Korea, the game achieved the status effectively (and briefly) of a national sport. It is rarely easy to chart the development of games outside the colonies, where the reasons for and methods of their introduction are not usually obvious. In the case of table tennis and the Far East Professor Tsuboi generally takes the blame; in the instances of Hungary, Austria, Czechoslovakia and Romania the British central European community, a loose but substantial social grouping before the First World War, is generally credited with having accidentally seeded 'whiff-whaff', 'gossima' and 'ping-pong' from about 1905 onwards through the medium of embassy dinner parties and the country house circuit of the fading old regime.

Whoever took this strange relic of Victorian parlour games to foreign parts can hardly have been aware of what they were planting. In 1926–27 the first World Table Tennis Championships for the Swaythling Cup were organised by the newly formed International Table Tennis Federation. For eight of its first nine years it was won by Hungary. The exceptional year saw Czechoslovakia lift it, and when Hungary finally released their grip in 1936, Austria took over. In the early 1950s Japan entered and commenced their own unbroken run of successes; before in their own turn giving way to China. Hungary also dominated the men's singles, men's doubles and women's doubles throughout the late 1920s and 1930s; the women's singles until Rozeanu of Romania took over between 1949 and 1955; and the mixed doubles until the Japanese ascendency of the 1950s. In the whole of this time England, the nanny of the sport, had perhaps just one truly memorable performer. Fred Perry, who would go on to become his country's only great male lawn tennis player of the twentieth century, won the men's singles at the World Championships in 1929.

Each of those games, and the racquet and ball game which was to become the biggest of them all, sprouted in their codified form from one stately root.

Real tennis, or royal tennis, or court tennis, was far from being a British invention. It evolved from medieval France and that game of 'jeu de paume' which led directly to Eton and Rugby Fives. Real tennis is mentioned in French ecclesiastical documents as early as the twelfth century, and by 1292 there were 13 makers of tennis balls registered in Paris. The lexicography of the game pays homage to these origins – in real tennis to this day parts of the court are named 'dedans', 'grille', 'tandour', and 'bandeau'. The word tennis itself apparently derives from the French call of *tenez* before serving; deuce is a corruption of *à deux*, meaning that the players needed two clear points to win. Even the scoring system of 15, 30, 40, game, which would be adopted by lawn tennis, came from medieval France. In the Europe of the Middle Ages the figure 60 had a significance similar to that of 100 in later times: the winner of a game of real tennis was consequently the first player to reach 60 in stages of 15 points, and somewhere down the line the score of 45 was corrupted into 40. 'Service', on the other hand, may have been an English term. It was certainly the practice at the time of Henry VIII, who ruled between 1509 and 1547, to employ a servant to throw the ball up and set a rally in motion: there was no consideration, in that era, of winning a point with the first stroke of the game.

Real tennis was played for centuries on a hard indoor court surrounded – like rackets or squash – by walls which were part of the playing area. Three of them, one side wall and the two at either end, were usually high and solid; the fourth, the other side wall, was often open to the light or, in artificially illuminated indoor arenas, it might open on to the spectators' gallery. It was played on flagstones chiefly because the old balls stuffed with hair and bound tightly with cloth would not bounce on grass. Not until the 1870s and the development, in Britain, of a ball made from rubber was this difficulty overcome.

It spread quickly to Britain, in the years when the crowned head of that country had also claims on the throne of France. In 1396 there was a prosecution at Canterbury for the offence of playing tennis. Just 18 years later the Dauphin made the mortal error of sending insulting tennis balls to the new King Henry V. This infamous sneer had the incidental effect of providing sports historians with the information that, by the late 1590s, William Shakespeare was familiar not only with the game of court tennis, but also with many of its finer points, for he had Henry reply:

> When we have matched our rackets to these balls,
> We will in France, by God's grace, play a set,

Shall strike his father's crown into the hazard.
Tell him, he hath made a match with such a wrangler,
That all the courts of France will be disturbed
With chases.

Rackets, sets, matches, courts and balls are self-explanatory puns; the hazard was a winning opening shot; and the chase was a complex form of scoring according to the nature of the ball's bounce after striking the back wall. A wrangler had in the 1590s nothing exclusively to do with sport: it meant simply a brawler.

One year later, in 1415, the Dauphin received his dues at the battle of Agincourt. One of his nephews, Prince Charles d'Orleans, was taken prisoner by the English at that action and was incarcerated in Wingfield Castle, where he reputedly taught the game of court tennis to the young men of his jailers, the Wingfield family. Their surname is worth remembering.

(Tennis was not, incidentally, an altogether fortunate game for the French monarchy. In 1316 Louis X died from drinking too much cold water after playing a game in the Forest of Vincennes; in 1498 Charles VIII perished after striking his head on the lintel of a door leading to a court at Amboise; and in 1789 the French Third Estate, locked out of the States-General by royal command, took its historic oath to insist upon a constitution, the oath which kick-started the French Revolution and set in motion the events which led to the decapitation of Louis XVI, on the real tennis court at Versailles.)

It is possible that, thanks to the Auld Alliance, crude early forms of real tennis were welcomed in Scotland while English monarchs still considered gifts of tennis balls to be demeaning jibes against a man's masculinity. Certainly, in the sixteenth century a game called 'caitch' was commonplace in Lanark. In 1598 James VI of Scotland, five years before he became James I of England, recommended 'le cache' to his eldest son, Prince Henry. It was similar to jeu de paume and was still alive, if faltering, as late as 1870, by which time it was known as handy. Caitch, le cache, or handy, was played between two teams of six, eight or ten a side, and according to a contemporary:

The game was for one man of each team alternately to strike the ball back to the wall with his hand, and the side which first failed to send it back lost one, which the other gained. And don't run away with the idea this was the innocent play this looks on paper. There were creases right and left perpendicularly, and above and below horizontally outside which the ball could not strike to count. There were clever fellows who could make it rebound from the wall thirty or forty feet as neatly as if cut; and there were sometimes cleverer ones who could send it back all that distance low enough to touch the wall just inside the lower crease. Men stripped to the work, and rolled up their shirt sleeves on their stout arms, and swung and sweat over it to a discipline as exacting as anything which prevails on the cricket field or amongst football players; to be the best handy player of a district was to be a hero.

But the courtly version of real tennis was, from the Middle Ages onwards, predominantly a game for the nobility. Throughout the sixteenth century the great and the good of France, England and Scotland vied with each other to produce more and better tennis courts. Henry VII of England played in courts at Woodstock, Windsor, Wycombe, Westminster and Sheen. When in 1506 Philip I of Castile was forced by the weather into Weymouth harbour, thus breaking his journey to claim the throne of the Netherlands, the Spaniard was entertained at Windsor by Henry VII and reportedly played a set of tennis with the Marquis of Dorset. Philip won easily, apparently because the marquis was using his hand – 'but the Kyng of Casteele played with the Rackete and gave the Lord Marques XV'. In 1530 both François I of France and Henry VIII of England built courts, at the Louvre and Hampton Court respectively, and in 1539 James V of Scotland countered with an open-air arena at Falkland Palace. Henry, if not James, had something of a pique for their French cousin. 'He is,' the oleaginous Venetian ambassador Sebastian Giustiniani wrote openly of the 29-year-old Henry VIII in 1519, 'much handsomer than any other sovereign in Christendom; a great deal handsomer than the King of France; very fair, and his whole frame admirable proportioned. On hearing that François I wore a beard he allowed his to grow, and as it is reddish, he has now got a beard which looks like gold. He is extremely fond of tennis, at which game it is the prettiest thing in the world to see him play, his fair skin glowing through a skin of the finest texture.'

Henry may have edged François on looks, but in the contest to promote tennis France won at a canter. François I followed his court at the Louvre with one at Fontainebleau, and with encouragements to his nobles to build so many courts across the land that, according to a report of the Papal Legate, by 1596 there were 250 real tennis courts in Paris alone, and they provided employment to 7,000 people. And when this energetic monarch decided to build a ship to overshadow Henry VIII of England's *Great Harry*, he christened a 2,000-ton four-masted man-o'-war *La Grande Francoise*, and he built a tennis court on its upper deck. His successor Henri II took up the chase with vigour and built a court at the Louvre which was portrayed in a diagram in the first book ever to be written about tennis, *Trattato del Giuoco della Palla* by the Italian priest Antonio Scaino da Salo, which was written in 1555. The dimensions of the court, and even of the illustrated 'rachetta', are wonderfully timeless. Either could have been employed by a tennis player of 400 years later.

The sixteenth and seventeenth centuries were the golden age of this seminal sport. At the time of Charles I there were 14 courts in London, which are still commemorated by such addresses as Tennis Street in Southwark. His two sons, who became Charles II and James II, also patronised the game. Charles II built a new court in the grounds of Windsor Castle, and there is an etching of the eight-year-old James, racquet in hand and balls scattered carelessly at his feet, on the Brake court at Whitehall.

There are many such portraits from the golden age. An English children's encyclopaedia of 1658 depicts a doubles match in a covered arena, with a single rope slung loosely across the middle of the court and three solid side walls opening on to gallery windows on the fourth side. The title page of Charles Hulpeau's *Le Jeu Royal de la Paume* shows a doubles match at full tilt, with one player across the net having delivered a high forehand, which his opponents are attempting to retrieve, one with a right-handed backhand stroke, and the other with a left-handed forehand. But the greatest re-creation by far is to be found in an unattributed sixteenth-century Flemish representation in oils of the biblical story of the meeting of David and Bathsheba. In the right-hand foreground a nervous medieval King David is handing a messenger a note. Far away, beyond a lawn, an orchard and a maze, where blue castellated ridges hover over an azure sea and ships put in to a busy harbour, the object of his summons sits washing her feet in an artificial pool, and is handed an earlier note by an earlier messenger.

There are many other people around at this notable moment in time, but none of them is paying any attention to the king's agitated wooing. They are instead watching a game of tennis. It is taking place on a roofless outdoor court in the immediate central foreground of the painting. Two men in tights and loose blouses are smacking a white ball about; three other balls lie discarded on the marked ground. Four men are watching from a bench at courtside; one peers through a grille in the door; five are leaning over the low court wall; and two more gaze raptly from a balcony while King David, virtually alone in his wilful ignorance of the game at hand, presses home his suit. They were never wrong, the old masters . . .

By the eighteenth century real tennis was declining both in France and in Britain. In 1657 the Dutch ambassador to Paris reported that the city's 250 tennis courts of just 60 years earlier had declined to 114. By 1783 there were just 13, and after that declaration in one of the 13 in 1789, France had things on its mind other than the vain pursuits of idle kings. In Britain, the Hanoverians never much liked games. The residual aristocratic tennis lobby allowed itself a glimmer of hope when the rebellious eldest son of George II, Frederick the Prince of Wales, took up the sport, but he died in 1751, some said following a blow from a tennis ball, and the hope died.

It was nonetheless the British who sustained real tennis. Napoleon Bonaparte was known to play the game on the court built by François I at Fontainebleau, but in post-revolutionary France it slowly died, and by 1960 there were just two courts remaining in use in that country, only one of which, at Bordeaux, had been built before the twentieth century. In the same year, 1960, there were 16 real tennis courts in Britain, three of them surviving from the sixteenth century, and nine of them built during the reign of Queen Victoria. There was also the court at 45 Davey Street, Hobart, Tasmania, which had been erected in 1875 by the retired English merchant Samuel Smith Travers for the benefit of his large family; and the court on Melbourne's Exhibition Road which was opened in April 1882 by the governor of the Australian state of Victoria, the Marquis of Normanby . . .

Fast, exciting and venerable as the game was in its own right, the principal historical function of real tennis was to give birth, in Great Britain, to one of the greatest games of the twentieth century. It started quietly enough. In the December of 1873 a member of the Honourable Corps of Gentlemen-at-Arms at the Court of Queen Victoria, a retired officer of the Guards named Major Walter Clopton Wingfield JP, was knocking a tennis ball around in the open air while house-partying with friends at Nantclwyd Hall at Llanelidan in Clwyd, Wales. It was not the first time that Walter Wingfield had enjoyed this outdoor version of real tennis, and it was far from being the first time that such a pursuit had delighted the Victorian British.

Major Harry Gem, a solicitor and clerk to the Birmingham magistrates, and a Spanish friend named J.B. Perera had marked out a rectangular tennis court on a lawn in Edgbaston as early as 1858. In 1869 Walter Wingfield himself was playing lawn tennis over a net two feet high at Lansdowne House in London. In 1872 Major Gem and J.B. Perera, together with two local doctors, established the first lawn tennis club at the Manor House Hotel in Leamington Spa. Those are solid, verifiable historical details; it is not necessary to speculate about all of the references to 'field tennis' and 'long tennis' which had occurred in sporting literature over the previous hundred years and more.

But there are reasons why the bust of Major Walter Clopton Wingfield, and not that of Major Gem, or of Señor Perera, or of a score of others who had hit a tennis ball outdoors, would come to occupy its proud position in the entrance hall of the Lawn Tennis Association's headquarters in London. The first of them was that Wingfield considered himself to be a man with an historical mission. He was, as he frequently reminded himself and others (chiefly through his conspicuous wearing of an Elizabethan doublet), a direct descendant of those young men of Wingfield Castle who had apparently been taught court tennis by their prisoner Charles d'Orleans in 1415 and 1416.

The second reason is that when Walter Wingfield found himself playing tennis yet again on the lawns of Nantclwyd Hall in December 1873, it is clear that the 'party assembled' in those chilly Welsh wealds – the party to whom he would later dedicate his book on the game – helped him to clarify and formulate a standard, simple and marketable set of rules and equipment.

He wasted no time in executing the third deed. Just two months after the gathering in Clwyd, on 23 February 1874, Walter Clopton Wingfield of Belgrave Road, Pimlico, applied to patent 'the invention of A New and Improved Portable Court for Playing the Ancient Game of Tennis . . . the object and intention of this Invention consists in constructing a portable court by means of which the ancient game of tennis is much simplified, can be played in the open air, and dispenses with the necessity of having special courts erected for that purpose.'

A month later, in March 1874, Walter Wingfield published the first edition of his booklet on the game. He did not, at that time, call it lawn tennis. He christened it 'sphairistike'. The word is Greek for 'ball game', and Wingfield's use of it indicates not only that he was a classical scholar and that he expected all patrons of his invention to be classical scholars. It also suggests that Walter Clopton Wingfield, descendant of the Wingfields of Wingfield Castle, was a student of the history of tennis, for that children's encyclopaedia of 1658 which had contained an illustration of doubles pairs playing court tennis in a covered arena had been annotated in Latin, and in its seventeenth-century dog-Latin the word devised for a tennis court had been 'sphaeristerio'.

Wingfield did not hold for long with sphairistike. The playful Victorians quickly abbreviated the word to 'sticky', which he considered to be frivolous and disrespectful. Hurt, he rechristened his patented invention 'lawn tennis'. In March 1874 *The Army and Navy Gazette* welcomed this creation by a son of the military with the words: 'A new game has just been patented by Major Wingfield, late 1st Dragoon Guards, which, if we mistake not, will become a national pastime. Lawn Tennis – for that is the name under which the game makes its appearance – is a clever adaptation of tennis to the exigencies of an ordinary lawn piece of ground.'

The game which Walter Wingfield put on the market in 1874 sold in a boxed set for five guineas. It comprised uncovered hollow india-rubber balls (which bounced on grass and were resistant to water), four racquets, netting and a set of instructions. Neophytes were advised to mark out an hourglass-shaped court 60 feet long, 30 feet wide at the baseline, and narrowing to 21 feet wide at the net, which was strung four feet eight inches from the ground. The server stood in a lozenge-shaped box and delivered into the opposite service court. The most obvious differences between Walter Wingfield's creation and its parent lay in the absence of walls, the consequent abandonment of such complex rules as the 'chase', which depended upon rebounds from the back walls, and in the shape of the court (real tennis being played, of course, on the straight rectangular court to which lawn tennis would later revert). In the March of 1875 the Marylebone Cricket Club, which doubled at that time as the governing body of rackets and real tennis, convened its (real) tennis committee to offer lawn tennis a set of rules. They increased the dimensions of Walter Wingfield's hourglass-shaped court and – with the inventor's benign approval, for he was flattered by the attention of such elevated people – they decided that the scoring system should be that of rackets rather than real tennis; in other words, it would be 15 up, with deuce at 14-all, and only the server scored.

It was an instant success. Wingfield's booklet on the game ran to five editions within a year, and in the fifth printing in 1875 he was able to boast that boxes of lawn tennis had already been bought by 11 princes and princesses, seven dukes, 14 marquises, three marchionesses, 54 earls, six countesses, 105 viscounts, 41 barons, 44 ladies, 44 honourables, five right honourables and 54 baronets and knights – 'quite a large segment,' the Australian tennis broadcaster Max Robertson would write, 'of Debrett and the Almanach de Gotha'. In total, between July 1874 and June 1875, Major Walter Clopton Wingfield sold 1,050 sets of tennis equipment – more than a third of them, by his own estimation, having gone to the aristocracy.

Lawn tennis spread overseas like a gospel. The home of Sir Brownlow and Lady Grey at Cleremont, Bermuda, had contained a tennis court in the year 1873, before Wingfield's epiphany at Nantclwyd. But only in 1874, when boxed sets of equipment began to arrive in the colony, did the British Bermudan garrison take up the game in earnest. An American visitor named Mary Ewing Outerbridge sampled the sport there and took one of Wingfield's packages with her back to New York, where her brother, A. Emilius Outerbridge, would lay down a court in the grounds of the Staten Island Cricket and Baseball Club. In the August of 1874, when the ink was hardly dry on Wingfield's patent, James Dwight and F.R. Sears unpacked an imported box of racquets, net and balls on a damp Massachusetts sward by the home of William Appleton at Nahant, Boston; and precisely two years later a club competition was held at Nahant. In 1880 the Staten Island Cricket and Baseball Club staged its own lawn tennis tournament at New Brighton, and by 1881 the United States Lawn Tennis Association had been formed, and the first official American championships were staged at the Rhode Island courts of the Newport Tennis Club.

In 1878 the Melbourne Cricket Club in Australia founded the MCC Lawn Tennis Club and laid the first asphalt tennis court in the colonies. The Sydney Cricket Club followed suit in 1880, founding the Sydney Lawn Tennis Club, and the first New South Wales championships; the first inter-colonial challenge matches between Victoria and NSW were both staged in 1885. They were followed by state competitions in Queensland in 1889, Tasmania in 1893 and Western Australia in 1895.

By 1875 the game was also to be found in Ireland, Scotland, Brazil, India, France and Germany. The first men's doubles competitions were held in Scotland in 1878, the Irish championships were launched in 1879, the Punjab Lawn Tennis Championships were first held in 1885, and the South African and German championships in 1892. In 1875 the remorselessly sporting Frederick Temple Hamilton-Temple, the Earl of Dufferin and governor-general of Canada between 1872 and 1878, built a tennis court at his official residence of Rideau Hall in Ottawa, although lawn tennis turned out not to be one of Dufferin's favourite sports, and the court was shortly pressed into extramural service as a banquet hall. And in Colombo, the capital of the colony of Ceylon (as Sri Lanka was then named) the Pussellawa Lawn Tennis Club decreed in 1893 – its ninth year of existence – that on Sundays its courts would be closed during the hour of divine service at the Pussellawa Parish Church of England.

Lawn tennis was played in Panama in 1878. The Decimal Tennis Club was set up in Paris in 1977, and by the end of the 1870s British holidaymakers had taken it to Dinard, Le Touquet and St Moritz. In 1881 it was reported that a tournament – not just a game or a set, but a tournament – had taken place on the summit of Mount Olympus, which stands at more than 9,000 feet above the Mediterranean Sea.

There was never, in the whole history of sport, so speedy and so widespread a colonisation of foreign countries as that which was enjoyed by the game of lawn tennis in the few years after its invention and codification. This was largely due to Walter Wingfield's inspired adaptation of the medieval racquet and ball game. But it also owed a massive debt to another, rather odd little survival of French courtly life.

Croquet was antique. This Gallic recreation, which had consisted simply of striking a large wooden ball through a series of hoops, had arrived early in England in the shape of pall-mall, that game which bequeathed its name to two major London thoroughfares. In France it had usually been known as 'maille', or mallet, although it seems likely that the people of Normandy had christened it 'croquet', the word being their own dialectical term for the standard French *crochet*, or 'hook'.

Useful as the medieval French may have been at devising games, their descendants were patently hopeless at dressing them up for the requirements of the modern age. That was the stern and self-appointed task of the British. As croquet, this harmless diversion arrived in Victorian England in much the same fashion as would Walter Wingfield's 'invention' of lawn tennis. In 1857 a manufacturer put boxed sets of mallets, hoops, balls and printed rules on the market, and suddenly 'hardly a house with a lawn was without its croquet set'. There were, of course, an increasing number of houses with lawns in Britain in the second half of the nineteenth century. Croquet enjoyed sufficient popularity among the burgeoning middle classes for some of its jargon to become a bourgeois euphemism for dying ('pegging out' meant striking the central peg with the ball, and thereby finishing one's round). In 1862 the indefatigable chronicler of respectable England, Anthony Trollope, gave the game its first British literary reference in his novel *The Small House at Allington*. (He would repeat the tribute in *The Eustace Diamonds* in 1873 – there could be no better illustration of Miss Lucy Morris's sweet sociability than the fact that she 'knew every rule at croquet'.) In 1867, ten years after the sale of the first croquet set, a tournament was held at Evesham. There was a second championships at Moreton-on-the-Marsh a year later (they were won by Messrs C.E. Willis and W.H. Peel, who are consequently in the record books – to the confusion of the French – as the first international croquet champions). In that same year, 1868, the editor of *The Field* magazine, J.H. Walsh, called a meeting at his offices in The Strand which resulted in the formation of the grandly titled All England Croquet Club.

In 1870 the All England Croquet Club rented for £50 a year four greenfield acres close by the London and South Western Railway line, with the postal address of Worple Road, Wimbledon. Five years later they were in trouble. Croquet had not only failed to sustain its dynamic drive through the gardens of Great Britain; the game was actually in decline. Some people knew precisely where to place the blame. 'Croquet was all very well in its way,' wrote the chairman of the two-year-old Lawn Tennis Association H.W.W. Wilberforce in the 1890 edition of the *Handbook of Athletic Sports*, 'but it gave no exercise; its social advantages are equally shared by lawn tennis; and it fostered (and for this reason principally it fell) the ascendancy of the curate.'

Wilberforce's last point, cryptic to a reader of a century later, was merely a dig by a Victorian public-school hearty at the perceived effeminacy of the younger clergy. His first two arguments were more widely shared. The sensational spread of lawn tennis eclipsed croquet. By 1875 the All England Croquet Club's rental on its four acres of Wimbledon had risen to £100, not many people were signing up to play croquet, and it was consequently financially embarrassed.

There was a boardroom coup. In 1875 one of the croquet club's founders, Henry Jones, won agreement for his suggestion that tennis should share the lawns at Worple Road with croquet. Tennis proved instantly to be more attractive than croquet, and in 1877 the club's name was changed to the All England Croquet and Lawn Tennis Club, and all those who still insisted on playing croquet alone were peremptorily ousted from the committee. The final ignominy came in 1882, when the Worple Road club dropped the word croquet altogether from its title as well as from its activities, and became for ever the All England Lawn Tennis Club.

Croquet would survive, if not thrive, thanks to the multiplicity of interests within the communities of the British Empire. The game was shakily resurrected in England in 1896 by W.H. Peel, the ageing victor of that second World Championships at Moreton-on-the-Marsh back in 1868. Peel founded the All England Croquet Association, and by 1900, although Peel was dead, it had accumulated 508 members and a playing area at Sheen House.

But in the antipodes croquet may never have required resuscitation, because there it seems never to have collapsed. There was a croquet club at Kyneton in Victoria as early as 1866. We have a photograph of four bonneted, bloused and bustled ladies scattered decoratively around croquet hoops at Angeston, South Australia in 1867. Two men stand langourously by, one with a mallet slung over his shoulder. By the close of the twentieth century the game was healthier in New Zealand than anywhere in the Northern Hemisphere, and Australia contained over 6,000 registered croquet players, which was more than any other country in the world. It is possible, but only possible, that in that distant continent people were able to appreciate croquet as an intricate and fascinating diversion in its own right, untainted by the associations with country-house pretensions and horsey, braying men and women which became increasingly unpopular in Great Britain as the people's century progressed.

In God's grand scheme for sport on earth, however, croquet, like real tennis, had been sacrificed on the altar of lawn tennis. The first two would stumble into and through the twentieth century, but the latter would take the age of change by storm. In 1877 the All England Club, which was by no means out of its financial quagmire, needed to raise money for a new pony roller. That Judas Iscariot of croquet Henry Jones suggested to his fellow turncoat J.H. Walsh of *The Field* that it might be a good idea to stage a men's tennis championships. Walsh agreed to put up a 25-guinea trophy, and on 9 June 1877 the following notice appeared in *The Field*:

The All England Croquet and Lawn Tennis Club, Wimbledon, propose to hold a lawn tennis meeting, open to all amateurs, on Monday July 9th, and following days. Entrance fee £1 1s. Two prizes will be given, one gold champion prize to the winner, one silver to the second player . . . players must provide their own rackets and shoes without heels.

It was the event which, as Max Robertson noted, transformed tennis from a pastime into a sport. All the games which were codified by the British had to endure this rite of passage: it became a well-trodden route from the establishment of the club, to the drawing-up of rules, to the holding of an open (although usually amateur) competitive championship. The first offered stability, the second provided common competitive ground, and the third, the red meat of contention, brought the sport to life. The All England Club gave all of those things to lawn tennis. Before its first championships it adjusted the MCC and Major Wingfield's rules. The hourglass-shaped playing area was scrapped and rectangular courts were marked out, the 15–30–40–game system of real tennis scoring replaced the 15-up of rackets, and the server was allowed one fault.

Twenty-two men entered the first Wimbledon tournament, paying a combined fee of 22 guineas, which meant that J.H. Walsh would have more obviously benefited the All England Club's pony roller fund in 1877 by giving the money spent on his 25-guinea trophy directly to the treasurer.

At first it may have been dispiriting. Only 200 spectators turned up for the final. The winner in 1877, a 27-year-old Old Harrovian named Spencer W. Gore who had been brought up on rackets, detested the real tennis scoring system, 'which was then for the first time introduced and which puzzled us "pretty considerable"'. Gore's contempt for the game of which he was the first champion would be undiminished by the passing years. In 1890, by which time the Wimbledon championships were drawing 3,500 spectators to the men's finals, the South Western Railway Company was stopping special trains at a halt by the courts during Wimbledon week, touts were selling, for half a sovereign each, building bricks upon which latecomers might stand to get a better view, a new lease had been taken out on the Worple Road grounds, and the club had found itself able not only to buy a new pony roller, but also to build a new clubhouse at a cost of £450. In 1890 Spencer Gore would write:

> . . . it is its want of variety that will prevent lawn tennis in its present form from taking rank among our great games . . . That anyone who has really played well at cricket, [real] tennis, or even rackets, will ever seriously give his attention to lawn tennis, beyond showing himself a promising player, is extremely doubtful: for in all probability the monotony of the game as compared with the others would choke him off before he had time to excel in it.

In the second Wimbledon final in 1878 Spencer Gore – who as defending champion was given a bye all the way to the last game (a tradition which lasted until 1921) – was beaten by P.F. Hadow. Hadow was a walking exemplar of the sporting empire. He was a planter at home from Ceylon for the summer. He took up the new game for the first time a few weeks before Wimbledon, entered the tournament, won it – and then sailed back to Ceylon and never thereafter so much as watched a game of tennis until 1926, when he was coaxed back to the All England Club's silver jubilee celebrations.

Both men were to be excused their indifference. As early as the late 1870s British tennis players were busily engaged in perfecting – and then introducing to America, France and Australia – the overhead serve and the smash. Rallies, those lengthy exhibitions of fitness and deft stroke play which men like Spencer Gore valued in real tennis and rackets, were yearly shortening on the grass of Wimbledon and on the basalt, cinder, sand and tarmacadam lawn tennis courts of the Empire.

But the game had taken root. It would occasionally subside, but never collapse. Lawn tennis, the game invented as a diversion for the Victorian aristocracy and upper middle classes, would become one of the British Empire's four most successful sporting exports. Its players would gradually come to contradict the scepticism of such as Spencer Gore, and see their game as a rich and integral part of the imperial tapestry. Eustace H. Miles, a less exalted tennis champion, would come to claim that the best proof of fitness to govern India was to have been a captain of games – 'It would be terrible,' Miles wrote, 'to think of what would happen to us if our public school system were swept away, or if – and this comes to very much the same thing – from our public school system were swept away our Athletics and our Games.'

And as tennis wandered the world in the company of administrators from the British public schools, the players from the country of its birth lost their grip on its trophies. Before 1907, when the Australian Norman Brookes won the first of his two Wimbledon titles, no non-Briton had done so. After 1936, when Fred Perry won the last of his three, no British man would repeat the feat. There were many reasons, but the efforts of President Franklin Delano Roosevelt are not to be overlooked. While Perry was collecting his trophies, Roosevelt's New Deal work crews were busily constructing 8,000 public lawn tennis courts across the length and breadth of the United States of America: an act of civic munificence which would double the number of tennis players (and, no doubt, spectators) in that country. The racquet and ball game had travelled far from Wingfield Castle in 1416.

If it seemed at times as if the citizens of the British Empire spent most of their waking hours devising and playing games; that is because many of them did. Three hundred British graduates were appointed to the Sudan Political Service during its 56 years of existence, and 93 of them were full Oxford or Cambridge blues. The Sudan – 'a land of blacks ruled by blues' – also boasted among its chief civil secretaries a Cambridge fencing blue, an Olympic oarsman and an Oxford rugby blue. When the recreations of 150 British governors of African colonies up until 1960 were surveyed, it was discovered that more than half of them had informed *Who's Who* that sport was their favourite means of relaxation.

It was not so much that sportsmen were favoured for those posts, although the ability to keep a straight bat was, by the last quarter of the nineteenth century, regarded, as we shall see, as something more than mere sporting technique. The fact was that sport had come absolutely to dominate the leisure hours of all British classes. Those games were not codified entirely from a sense of duty; clubs were not always joined for reasons of social advantage; the games were often played and refined for the joy of it. In other words, it would have been difficult, at the end of the nineteenth century, to find a random sample of 300 British graduates which did not include 93 sporting fanatics. The wonder is that the percentage was so small.

They were attracted to sport, just as they were attracted to empire. In both cases they were pioneers. The early player of tennis or soccer or rugger could shape his sport and leave his mark upon it, as plainly as an enthusiastic district commissioner could realistically hope to mould a part of Africa in his own image. The relationship between sport and empire became increasingly symbiotic as the Empire swelled towards its fullest girth in the 1920s and 1930s. The confidence of one fed off the confidence of the other; they came to share not only the common goals of healthy Christian minds within healthy Christian bodies, but also vocabularies (with phrases such as 'common goals') and structures. There could be no man better suited to the chairmanship of a local athletics club than a retired district officer or Indian Army major. They were accustomed to command, to discipline, and to order. Men who had imposed codes and standards upon alien territories the size of Great Britain were unlikely to condone disorder and indiscipline at a running meet. And in time even the ideologies of sport and empire would become hopelessly entangled.

Sport was not an incidental of the British Empire; sport was at the heart of the matter. The same urges which drove the Victorians and Edwardians to explore and then to order the world, persuaded them to seek out and codify its recreations; the same genius which was involved in creating games which would increase in popularity over the following hundred years and more, was also involved in developing the steamboat, the submarine telegraph cable and the suspension bridge.

Colonel Sir Neville Chamberlain, who bore no relation to the British prime minister of the same name, is not so celebrated as James Watt or Thomas Telford. Chamberlain's contribution to western civilisation was nonetheless large, and enormously popular, and widespread, and lasting. As a young subaltern with the Devonshire Regiment, Neville Chamberlain found himself stationed at Jubbulpore in British India in 1875. During the rainy season which rendered polo and rugger and cricket impractical, Chamberlain's fellow officers resorted to the billiards table.

A form of billiards had arrived in Britain from France by the sixteenth century. The French thereafter lost control of this game as well as of tennis. Perhaps they deserved to. While the British assiduously converted billiards into an excellent indoor betting sport which required substantial skills, the French were turning it into an early form of novelty golf by placing hoops and small fortresses on the tables, calling it 'Le Royal Jeu des Fortifications', and obdurately resisting the British innovation of pockets at each corner and down two sides of the table.

If the game requires a patrimony, there is no shortage of historical references to British billiards. In 1576 the imprisoned Mary, Queen of Scots, complained of the 'cruel way in which she had been deprived of her billiard table'. Spenser and Chapman refer to the pastime, and in 1605 James I of England and VI of Scotland ordered for his personal use a 'billiarde bourde twelve foote longe and fower foote broade, the frame being walnutte'. Shakespeare had Cleopatra, who was unlikely to have been familiar with the game, suggest 'let us to billiards', and the poet Charles Cotton in 1674 described billiards in detail in *The Compleat Gamester*.

By the start of the nineteenth century John Thurston had begun to manufacture billiards tables in The Strand. In 1834 and 1835 Thurston replaced the traditional oak bed with slate and replaced the felt cushions with rubber – that product which was newly available from the colonies and which would change the shape of so many imperial sports. A Thurston table was a gorgeous thing: 'A very superior 12-foot Gothic Billiard Table,' announced one advertisement, 'with clustered columns, caps and bases, handsome carved ornaments in corners, carved cusps and pendants, cushions to form a moulded weather table with frieze, embossed with various flowers, crests and shields – the whole of the finest flowery wainscot, £150.' In 1845 John Thurston surpassed himself by acquiring some of the oak from the man-o'-war *Royal George*, which had sunk off Spithead in 1772, building a billiards table from it, installing the first set of vulcanised rubber cushions, and presenting the finished item to Queen Victoria at Windsor Castle.

Thurston's name would live on, chiefly thanks to the billiards den Thurston's Hall, which operated in Leicester Square from 1901 to 1955. 'When the world is wrong, hardly to be endured,' wrote J.B. Priestley, 'I shall return to Thurston's and there smoke a pipe among the connoisseurs of top and side. It is as near to the Isle of Innisfree as we get within a hundred leagues of Leicester Square.'

John Thurston's influence was most marked during his own lifetime, however, for it was then, in the first half of the nineteenth century, that his perfect tables guaranteed a smooth run of the ball and a consistent response from the cushions. And it was then that the early Victorians devised a roomful of variations on the billiards theme. Shell-out, pyramids, skittle pool, black pool, caroline, doublet – all provided different betting opportunities, and all provided a comfortable living for the pool-room sharks which lurked in those dark waters.

Those were the games with which Subaltern Neville Chamberlain and his fellows whiled away the monsoon afternoons at Jubbulpore in 1875. They were familiar with pyramids, which required 15 red balls to be placed in a triangle, and the opponents to bet on each red as it was nominated by the player. They knew life pool, in which each player had a separate object ball and cue ball. If his cue ball was potted by an opponent he lost one of four lives and had to pay a stake. They would have played black pool, where the player who had potted his object ball could then have an attempt at the black. If he sunk it he won more money and could then prolong his break by trying for the nearest red ball. The armies of the east were intensely familiar with billiards cues. Every serving officer knew that one of their number, the enormous Captain Frederick Gustavus Barnaby of the Royal Horse Guards, who as well as being a famous eastern adventurer was reputed to be the strongest man in the British army, would prove his power by grasping the tip of a cue between his middle and index fingers and holding it out horizontally, 'his arm fully extended and the butt end steady'.

Neville Chamberlain might also, in that monsoon season of 1875, have been aware of a game which had been played on the billiards tables of the Garrick Club in London since the 1860s. This involved several coloured balls as well as a pyramid of reds, and insisted upon the idiosyncratic (and sadly since abandoned) rule: 'In the event of the yellow ball being involved in a foul stroke, it is the custom for the watchers to cry out the word "bollocks!"'

In India Chamberlain devised a game which involved 15 red object balls, one each of yellow, green, pink and black, and one shared cue ball. The differently coloured object balls were given different values, which added to the betting opportunities. The name of the game arrived shortly afterwards. Sixty-three years later, in 1938, Colonel Sir Neville Chamberlain told the writer Compton Mackenzie (who was himself so great a fan of billiards and pool that he had a full-sized table transported to and installed in his remote Hebridean home on the island of Barra) that the Devonshire Regiment had received a visit one day from another young subaltern who had trained at the Royal Military Academy in Woolwich. This subaltern chanced to remark that at Woolwich the contemptuous name for a first-year cadet was a 'snooker', a casual corruption of *neux*, the French word for a novice which the British officers of the day pronounced 'nooks', and which also led to their dismissive expression for a youngster, 'snooks'.

> The term was a new one to me [recalled Chamberlain in 1938] but I soon had the opportunity of exploiting it when one of our party failed to hole a coloured ball which was close to the corner

pocket. I called out to him: 'Why, you're a regular snooker.' I had to explain to the company the definition of the word, and to soothe the feelings of the culprit I added that we were all, so to speak, snookers at the game, so it would be very appropriate to call the game snooker. The suggestion was adopted with enthusiasm and the game has been called snooker ever since.

Snooker was a purely imperial product. It was fathered by the imperial military, it would be fostered in a supremely imperial home, and it would be adopted and shown to the world by a travelling imperial sportsman.

Neville Chamberlain left the Devons in 1876 and joined the 12th Lancers, introducing snooker to their mess at Bangalore. He was then injured in the second Afghan War of 1878–81, and moved for rest and recreation to the hill station of Ootacamund in southern India. There, at 'snooty Ooty', the very quintessence of the British Raj, snooker became the recreation of the day. The Ootacamund Club would later dubiously proclaim itself to be the nursery of Neville Chamberlain's inspiration. The rules of the game were drawn up and hung in its billiards room, which was preserved into the twentieth century as a kind of snooker shrine. The diversion which a hundred years later would have become easily the most popular of all of the children of billiards, and which would be mastered and dominated by the working class, was an adopted baby of the imperial aristocracy.

The snooker room at Ootacamund was described by Trevor Fishlock in *The Times*:

> It is entered through a door properly fitted with a peephole, marked 'Wait For Stroke', so that you do not in ungentlemanly fashion cause distress at the table. The room has ceiling beams and white walls hung with the skulls and heads of 19 beasts and with large pictures of the Defence of Rorke's Drift, the Retreat from Moscow, the Battle of Tel el-Kabir and the Charge of the Light Brigade. It has a handsome table over which, if you are fortunate, you may be permitted to lean and sight your cue almost as a kind of obeisance. The room's furnishings are redolent of leisured snookery evenings, joshing and cigar smoke, as the balls click, spin and glide across the faded baize. On the wall near the cue rack there are framed accounts and letters testifying to the origin of the game and its curious name.

Had the story ended at Ootacamund, snooker might never have become a game whose 1985 world championships would attract the largest British audience for a televised sporting event, the largest BBC2 audience ever recorded, and the largest British post-midnight viewing figures (18.5 million saw Dennis Taylor beat Steve Davis by 18 frames to 17), and which before the close of the twentieth century was being played at the highest level in Malta, Thailand, the Philippines and Belgium, as well as in all of the former white dominions.

It did not end at Ootacamund because during the 1880s the greatest billiards player of his day, John Roberts junior, was touring the Empire. Roberts would cultivate this international circuit with enormous success. He played in the Australian outback and in Chicago music halls, but his best returns came from India. There, he once chartered elephants to carry a billiards table to show to the Maharajah of Jaipur. The Maharajah was entranced. He ordered half a dozen of them, and created John Roberts 'Billiards Player for Life at the Court of Jaipur'. Roberts would be paid £500 annually, with full expenses, for travelling to India once a year. At Jaipur he and his wife were housed in a palace of their own with 100 servants. In return for these considerations, Roberts taught billiards to the Maharajah and arranged local tournaments.

Roberts also opened a billiards table factory in Calcutta, and was dining there with the Maharajah of Cooch Behar when that gentle-man, who was also a billiards enthusiast, showed him a handwritten copy of the rules of snooker. Roberts expressed an interest, and the ruler of Cooch Behar then introduced him to Neville Chamberlain. Snooker became a part of John Roberts's peripatetic repertoire. The road to Thurstons in Leicester Square, to the Sheffield Crucible, and to 18.5 million people staying up past midnight to watch the game, was open.

Nothing escaped the disciplined eye of the Victorian sportsman. In 1865 a 40-year-old London Scot named John MacGregor, who was predictably nicknamed Rob Roy, returned to England from North America and promptly commissioned the boatbuilders Searle's of Lambeth to shape for him from oak and cedar a strange-looking craft which would be propelled by double-bladed paddles or, given a following wind, a small lugsail. These were called canoes, said John MacGregor, and he had seen them 'in North America and the Kamschatka'.

126

MacGregor immediately set off in his first canoe, which he named 'Rob Roy' after himself and his celebrated fellow clansman, for a tour of Europe's rivers and lakes. Upon his return he published a book titled *A Thousand Miles in the Rob Roy Canoe*. Within 12 months Searle's of Lambeth were manufacturing dozens more 'Rob Roys' to order, and in 1866 a meeting at the Star and Garter Hotel in Richmond resulted in the inauguration of the Canoe Club, whose founding objectives were those of 'improving canoes, promoting canoeing and uniting canoeists'. John MacGregor accepted the position of club captain, and in 1867 Edward the Prince of Wales became club commodore (and member number 57, with his canoe 'Risk'). A 15-canoe regatta was held on the Thames in the same year; John MacGregor made well-publicised voyages down the River Jordan and the Nile in 1867 and 1868; and in 1873 Queen Victoria commanded that the Canoe Club should become the Royal Canoe Club.

There was a Clyde Canoe Club by 1876, and in 1880 the art of canoeing was officially recognised on the continent of North America, where John MacGregor had first seen it practised, with the foundation in New York of the American Canoe Association. This body contained no native Americans. Following John MacGregor's death in 1892 the sport was driven chiefly by Europeans who had been introduced to the canoe by the young Victorian Britons who set out in the last quarter of the century to emulate MacGregor's famous feat of paddling through the continent. Thus it was an Austrian, H.W. Pawlata, who became in 1927 the first European to accomplish an Eskimo roll. He was taught the skill not by an Inuit, but by the study of learned papers on life in the frozen north. Three years later the Englishman Henry George 'Gino' Watkins did learn the Eskimo roll directly from its inventors: he travelled to Greenland in 1930 to explore the possibility of an Arctic air route to Canada for the Empire Airship Scheme, and while he was there he took to canoeing with the natives. (Watkins, one of the later imperial explorers, died at the age of just 25 while on a second trip to Greenland two years later, when his kayak overturned in an icy fjord.)

But by 1930 the centre of international canoeing was to be found in the centre of Europe. In 1924 the first International Canoe Federation was formed in Munich. In 1936 a party of English students, direct spiritual heirs to John 'Rob Roy' MacGregor, took a canoeing holiday in Bavaria. They were politely, if condescendingly and quite inaccurately, greeted by the DKV, the German canoeing authority, with the message: 'Rightly are the representatives of the Manchester Canoe Club styled England's Kayak pioneers; they stand but little behind the finest performers of Europe.'

The Empire was so far flung, and encompassed so many different climates and cultures that a multiformity of recreations were chanced upon by its sons and daughters – and a great diversity of conditions and appetites were available to the exporters of manufactured British games. Some of these games were duly shipped overseas not so much to improve the mental disciplines of colonials, as to cement the links between the British Abroad and the British at Home.

Curling, for example, which required a large playing area of frozen water, was never likely to catch on in Australia or South Africa before the development of artificial covered rinks. The first of those to be built in the world was the mechanically refrigerated rink called the Glacierium, which was created off the King's Road in London by John Gamgee in 1876, specifically for skating. Three years later, in 1879, the Southport Glacierium became the first artificial ice rink to introduce indoor curling. The Australian equivalent to those pioneering institutions, the Melbourne Glacierium, would not be opened until 1904.

But outdoor curling was heaven-sent to nineteenth-century Canada and the northern United States. This was one of the oldest of surviving British pursuits. Until the nineteenth century it was exclusively confined to the Netherlands, where it featured in the paintings of such as Pieter Bruegel, and to neighbouring Scotland, where the game was extensively lauded in rhyme. The physician and poet Alexander Pennecuik rhapsodised at the end of the seventeenth century:

> To Curle on the Ice does greatly please,
> Being a manly Scotish Exercise
> It Clears the Brains, stirs up the Native Heat,
> And gives a gallant Appetite for Meat.

Pennecuik's tribute was one of the earliest offered by a doctor to the health-giving qualities of sporting participation. Others, equally percipient, saw in curling the possibility of training a healthy mind within a healthy body. The versifier Alexander Boswell, the son of Samuel Johnson's biographer James, wrote early in the nineteenth century:

Rin to cards and to dice,
And gamblin, sit girnin and gurlin,
But honest men ken
That tho' slipp'ry the ice
Still fair-play an' fun gang wi' Curlin'.

As with the game of golf, there is no way of knowing whether the sport which involved sliding heavy stones towards a fixed target originated in Scotland or in the Netherlands. There is no doubt, however, who named the game, who developed it and gave it rules, or who took it around the world. The word 'curling' was found carved on a stone at Stirling dating from 1511. In 1716 the curlers of Kilsyth in Stirlingshire formed themselves into a club. At Wanlockhead high in the Lowther Hills it was boasted that the village's altitude, and consequently increased number of days when the temperature remained below freezing point, bred the best curlers in the world. The men of nearby Sanquhar disagreed and suggested that they personally would have to go to the moon to find their equals. 'Aye,' came the reply from further up the hill, 'but tell 'em to ca' at Wanlockhead on the way up.'

By 1807 at the latest, Scots had introduced curling to Canada, and in 1820 the Orchard Lakes Curling Club was formed at Pontiac in Michigan, USA. But the game's biggest leap forward took place in Scotland. John Cairnie, who had been born about 1769, spent his professional life as a surgeon in India before retiring to Largs in Scotland early in the nineteenth century. As a curling enthusiast he became frustrated by the number of days in which mild weather – even in Scotland – melted the ice on the ponds, and so Cairnie invented a shallow, clay-lined artificial pool which once frozen, stayed frozen for up to four times as long.

By way of thanks for this and other tokens of his devotion, when the first body which claimed international jurisdiction over the game, the Grand Caledonian Curling Club, was formed in Edinburgh in 1838, John Cairnie became its first chairman. He took curling to the Palace of Scone in 1842 to show Queen Victoria, as a result of which he found himself chairman of the Royal Caledonian Curling Club, with Prince Albert as his patron.

Curling was already an enormously popular sport in nineteenth-century Scotland. It would later be elbowed from prominence by the growth of other games which attracted the vast working class, but in the 1840s curling was the one sport which could truly claim to attract a whole nation at play.

And that is what John Cairnie's Royal Caledonian Curling Club set out to do in 1847. The first Grand Match was scheduled to be played between the north and the south of Scotland on 15 January in that year, on the upper pond at Penicuik House in Midlothian. Although one historian would comment that 'the 15th of January 1847 will be marked with a white stone in the chronicles of curling', the day was something of a failure. Only 12 rinks appeared from the north, and the vaster numbers from the south had to be sub-divided and asked to play among themselves.

A year later everything changed. Six thousand people – easily the greatest number of spectators ever to attend a sporting contest in Scotland – turned up at Linlithgow Loch on 25 January 1848 to watch 35 northern rinks take on 35 from the south, while an additional 100 rinks created a sideshow, an off-loch diversion.

That was the spectacle towards which most Victorian sports eventually aspired. It would be difficult 100 years later – difficult, indeed, 50 years later – to perceive curling as a forerunner of the mass spectator sport industry. But it was, as the accounts of witnesses to the events in the grounds of Linlithgow Palace on 25 January 1848 make clear. From before dawn thousands of players and enthusiasts 'might be observed pouring from all parts of the country, far and near, into the quiet town of Linlithgow; every train, both from east and west, as it arrived at the station, disgorging some hundred combatants, fully accoutred with stones and besoms [twig brooms].

> Numerous vehicles, besides, of all descriptions, loaded with passengers, came rattling in through every inlet to the town. From the position which we occupied, we had a very good opportunity of surveying the different groups as they arrived. First comes a band of strapping lads from the hills, with their plaids and broad blue bonnets, the very 'beau ideal' of Scottish peasantry. Next comes a party who, from the ruddy glow of their cheeks, and their big topcoats, are evidently south-country farmers, come up to fight for the honour of the Loudons. Here again is a lot of spruce-looking brethren of the rink, evidently from Edinburgh; they are the Merchiston Club, who have the honour to claim Prince Albert as a Member. Another train arrives with a fresh batch of curlers, among whom we distinguish the Noble President-Elect of the Royal Club, the Duke of Athole, at the head of his four rinks of Highlanders . . .

It is self-evident that without the overarching regulations of the self-appointed international governing body, the Royal Caledonian Curling Club, not only would those thousands of disparate people never have gathered together at the one frozen loch; but also they would not, once there, have been playing precisely the same game. Blair Atholl was, in 1848, a long way from the Loudons.

Half a century later, Nova Scotia was also a long way from Edinburgh. But in 1902, A. Davidson-Smith of the Royal Caledonian Curling Club was able to correspond with Gilbert John Murray Kynynmond Elliot, the fourth Earl of Minto, about sending the first Scottish curling team to Canada. Minto was at the time governor-general of that dominion (he would progress to the highest imperial office as viceroy of India between 1905 and 1910), and was the very model of his kind. The scion of a classically imperial family, his grandfather had been viceroy of Corsica and governor-general of India and his father had been an ambassador to Berlin and first lord of the Admiralty.

He believed that the British abroad were just that: brethren divided by a waste of sea but indissolubly bound by blood and culture. So when British troops fought Boers in the South African War, the fourth Earl of Minto ensured that Canadian men were there in uniform beside them. And when A. Davidson-Smith wrote to suggest that the visit to Canada of a touring group of Scottish curlers might further cement the imperial bond, Minto leapt at the idea.

It was irresistible. 'It is now strongly felt,' argued Davidson-Smith from Edinburgh, 'that in view of His Majesty the King's approaching Coronation and other recent events, together with the strong Imperial feeling as to the desirability and necessity of cementing the ties that unite the Mother Country with her Colonies, that the auspicious time has arrived when such a proposal should take effect.'

A trophy was put up for a Scottish/Canadian curling international by a grand old man of the empire. Donald Alexander Smith had first travelled to Canada from his native Scotland at the age of 18 in 1838, when he became a Hudson's Bay Company clerk. By 1868 he was the head of the company's Montreal department; he went on to play a huge role in the completion of the Great Northern and Canadian Pacific Railways; he became the governor of the Hudson's Bay Company in 1889; high commissioner for Canada in 1896; and in 1897 he was made the first Baron Strathcona and Mount Royal – during which elevation he raised Strathcona's Horse to assist the British cause in the South African war.

Scotland's 24 visiting curlers lost that first Strathcona Cup match in 1903. But if there was a winner, it was considered by all, it was the Pax Britannica. The captain of the Scottish tourists, the Reverend Kerr, later reported an address given to his team upon their arrival by a Nova Scotian minister, Reverend W.T. Herridge. 'They felt,' Kerr said that Herridge said, 'as much as their Scottish brethren did that they were part of the British Empire, with their own part to play in the modelling of its destiny. He [Herridge] was convinced that the visit of the Scottish Curling Team would help to cement still more closely the bonds which united them, and that every interchange of a similar kind would strengthen the true Imperialistic sentiment, and make them quick to discern our essential unity.'

The logical progression of imperial thought was here quite evident: the Empire was a good and necessary thing; the Empire depended on white unity; and of all of the elements which bound white colonists to each other and to 'the Mother Country', sport was among the strongest.

That was how and why curling first became an international game. It did not, naturally, fade with the evening of imperial expansion. Sports, like the Empire which bred them, proved to have a momentum all of their own. By 1994 the World Curling Federation had 31 member countries in four continents (there were none in Africa, understandably, or in Antarctica despite the suitable terrain). Member countries included Andorra, Korea, Liechtenstein, Mexico, and the US Virgin Islands. When the WCF was first established in 1966 its inaugural president was Major Allan Cameron of the Royal Caledonian Curling Club. By 1994 the presidency had rotated through Canada and Sweden and the USA to Germany, but its permanent secretariat was fittingly sited in Edinburgh.

It was difficult for a British boy in Edwardian times to open his Christmas sporting annual at, say, the close of the year 1910, and discover a game for which his countrymen had not been, in some crucial manner, responsible. He may have been vaguely aware that a century earlier a hobby-horse had first been employed in Paris as a form of children's mock-transport (when it was still, in England, a wicker animal used in morris dancing). He probably did not know that a German, Baron von Drais, had introduced his new improved hobby-horse-with-wheels to London in 1818, and that he had christened this forerunner of the children's scooter the Draisenne and had had it manufactured in Long Acre.

But he could have guessed that it would take a Briton to invent the bicycle. This was Kirkpatrick Macmillan of Courthill, Dumfries, who in 1839 created a two-wheeled vehicle which was propelled by a treadle and a system of levers attached to the single rear wheel. Three years later Macmillan was fined in Glasgow for knocking a young girl over in the street (although the magistrate, after being fascinated by a demonstration of Macmillan's new machine in the courthouse yard, later refunded the fine out of his own pocket), and the history of cycling heard little more from this pioneering Scot. In 1861 a Parisian manufacturer of perambulators and invalid carriages named Pierre Michaux developed from a damaged Draisenne (which had been offered to his children) a front-wheel-driven, pedal-and-crank velocipede which became known in Britain as the 'bone-shaker', and which was eponymously named by its inventor the 'Michaux'. Like Kirkpatrick Macmillan, Michaux was soon left behind. Rowley B. Turner, who was the Parisian representative of the Coventry Sewing Machine Company, took a velocipede back home to England in 1868 and astonished Londoners by riding it over London Bridge and down Cheapside to Euston Station, where he took a train to Coventry. The men of the CSM firstly elevated the size of its front wheel, then diminished its rear wheel, then christened it the 'High Ordinary' (although it would become better known to the British public as the Penny Farthing), and put it into factory production.

That was the birth of the international cycling industry. This being Victorian England, the clubs, with their rules and constitutions, quickly followed − extremely quickly, in fact: the oldest cycling organisation in the world, the Pickwick Cycling Club, was founded at the death of Charles Dickens in 1870, just two years after Rowley Turner's introduction of the velocipede to his Coventry plant.

With the invention of the differential axle and the perfection of ball-bearings (further British wheezes, attributed to James Starley in 1877, which gave firstly bicycles and later motor cars an easy system of gearing) cycling became one of the most efficient means of transport devised by humans. The hobby spread around the world. A velocipede was built at Goulburn in New South Wales in 1867, one year before production began at Coventry, and an English Ordinary was exported to Melbourne in 1875 − leading to bicycle clubs in Melbourne (1878), Sydney (1879), Tasmania (1880), South Australia and Brisbane (both 1881), and Western Australia (1891). Across Europe and around the English-speaking and British-governed world, the bicycle became a contemporary phenomenon: releasing working men and women of all classes from the confines of their neighbourhoods and homes, and allowing for a new and bold form of speed-sport.

Remarkably, Britain held on to its hegemony over this international phenomenon for a number of decades. The Bicycle Union, which became the Cyclists' Touring Club, the oldest national cycling body, was established in 1878; the rear-chain driven 'bicyclette' was – despite its attractive French name – designed by an Englishman, H.J. Lawson, in 1879; in 1882 at the Crystal Palace H.L. Cortis became the first human being to pedal a High Ordinary at over 20mph. Ten years later, in 1893, British cyclists instituted the sport's first global governing body, the International Cycling Association, and the first World Championships were held. They were dominated then as later by continental Europeans; but it would be an American, Charles Murphy, who first pedalled a bike at over 60 mph in 1899. 'Mile-a-Minute' Murphy achieved his goal by cycling behind a train on a smooth wooden platform laid between 2.25 miles of the Long Island Railroad. A Briton would not achieve that speed until 1908; and it was the French who would, with their creation of the most prestigious distance road race in the world in 1903, reclaim their inventive Parisian heritage by elevating cycling most closely to the position of a national sport. Not that the British were left entirely to regret a game that got away . . . after all, the oldest road race in the world, the one first travelled in 1891 between Bordeaux and Paris, was won in its inaugural year by an Englishman, G.P. Mills, who completed the 357 miles in 26 hours, 34 minutes and 37 seconds . . . and the third oldest – and certainly the most pioneering – road race in the world was organised by the British Abroad, when A. Calder cycled the 165 miles between Warrnambool and Melbourne, Victoria, in 11 hours, 44 minutes and 30 seconds.

He had a lot of games to study, that British Edwardian boy, which is why of course he fell behind in some of them. He could reflect that the modern sport of fencing was effectively a British invention, as judicial duelling, which died in France in the middle of the sixteenth century, was kept alive in England until 1818. (François de Chataignerie and Guy de Jarnac reputedly contested the last French duel on 10 July 1547; before – and indeed after – its criminalisation in Britain in 1818, duelling with swords survived as a vaguely disreputable form of trial by fighting, its popular recreational variety having been overtaken, as we have seen, by men and women performing with swordsticks.) After the prohibition of serious duelling, the London Fencing Club was founded to promote the occupation as a sport in 1848, and in 1860 the British Army introduced fencing into its physical education training at Aldershot. In 1895 the Fencing Branch Committee of the Amateur Gymnastic Association was established. It published the first sporting rules for fencing a year later, and they became the foundations of the game's presence in the revived Olympic Games.

He could look at hockey, and consider yet another British colonisation of a Gallic notion: hockey being nothing more than the medieval French variety of the old Celtic bent-stick-and-ball game, an unmistakable courtly version of which has been found depicted on a panel of a silver and enamel cruet made in Paris as early as 1333.

But the post-revolutionary nineteenth-century French, as we have seen in the instances of tennis and billiards, were keener to reject their misspent past than to immortalise its games, and so hockey was left in the loving hands of the British. Members of the Teddington Cricket Club in Middlesex first played hockey with a hard round cricket ball on a flat broad cricket pitch, and by the early 1870s they had effectively reinvented the game. In 1886 the Teddington club and six others formed the Hockey Association and the first national rules were duly agreed upon. In 1895 the first international was played at Richmond in Surrey, between Britain and Ireland – for many of the young protestant gentlemen of that colony had eagerly adopted hockey in preference to its nationalist, Catholic cousin, hurling.

England won that first international easily, by 5–0. They would be less happy in the future company of another dominion. Hockey was taken to Calcutta by soldiers of the Raj in the 1880s. By the first decade of the twentieth century it was estimated that every college, high school and native regiment in the Punjab was playing the game better than were its European originators.

It took them a while to get the chance of proving it, but when they did the evidence became overwhelming. The British established the International Hockey Board in 1908, just in time for it to legislate for the introduction of hockey to the London Olympic Games. Only European teams entered, and England (who disposed of the hapless French 10–0 in a preliminary round) won the gold medal. Not until the Amsterdam Olympics of 1928 did India compete, and then, like Malaya in badminton and Egypt and Pakistan in squash, the Empire struck back. As the only non-European team entrant, India won the gold hockey medal at the first attempt. They held it four years later in

Los Angeles, by defeating Japan 11–1 and the USA 24–1; in Berlin in 1936 they beat the German hosts 8–1 in the final to record a hat-trick of hockey gold medals (and establish a national sporting hero in Major Dhyan Chand, who netted a double hat-trick in that final). In London in 1948 India met Great Britain for the first time in an international hockey match. India won by 4–0. She won again in 1952, and again in 1956 before being supplanted as Olympic champions in 1960, after 32 years and six competitions, by Pakistan.

And so, turning through the pages of his Edwardian annual, our impressionable child would uncover mounting evidence of this unusual form of imperialism. He might stumble across the young sport of motorcycling, whose first organisation, the Auto-Cycle Club, had been established just a few years ago, in 1902, in England; and whose first racing event, the London to Edinburgh run, had taken place in 1904. He might gaze with amazement upon an illustration of Charles Collier, the British auto-cyclist who had become the first Isle of Man Tourist Trophy holder in 1907 and who had, just a few months before that Christmas of 1910, broken the world record by averaging 50.63 mph over the Peel circuit on his Matchless auto-cycle.

He may have wondered if the sport of mountaineering, so very popular in that year of 1910, had really dated from the famous day back in 1854 when Alfred Wills hired some villagers of Grindelwald in the Swiss Alps to escort him to the 12,000-foot summit of the Wetterhorn – not for reasons of scientific or geographical or geological research, or to hunt animals and plants, as so many had climbed before, but purely and simply because the Englishman Alfred Wills wanted to go there: he desired to achieve the ascent for its own sake. Was that why the Alpine Club had been formed in London in 1857? To cater for the purely British obsession with – as one of the most celebrated of their own number, the ill-starred George Leigh Mallory, would later suggest – climbing hills just because they were there? Was that why Edward Whymper led the first ascents of several peaks of the Mont Blanc chain in 1864, of Aiguille Verte in 1865, and finally, and with most chilling resonance (for four of his party were killed in this adventure, and Queen Victoria inquired after it whether mountain climbing could be made illegal), of the Matterhorn in July 1865?

In the last century of the British Empire, a century of which our Edwardian boy finds himself directly in the middle, climbing would become not so much an imperial sport as an imperial metaphor for a world awaiting conquest. The last great deed of empire, if not of imperial sporting achievement, came at its end, when on the evening of the coronation of Queen Elizabeth II in June 1953 a New Zealander named Edmund Hillary and a Nepalese named Sirdar Tenzing, climbing under the direction of Colonel John Hunt, a British army officer, reached the summit of the highest mountain in the world. That mountain had been named back in 1849 after a former Surveyor-General of British India, Sir George Everest. (The Tibetans still know it as Chomolungma, which means either 'Goddess Mother of the World' or 'Lady Cow'; and before 1849 the British had called it, more prosaically, Peak XV.) Hillary and Tenzing returned from their conquest to report victory to Colonel Hunt in Camp IV, in the presence of a young writer named James Morris who would become one of the finest chroniclers of the imperial romance, and who would report that day to *The Times* of this last and most emblematic feat of empire that 'Tenzing spent the fifteen minutes on the summit eating mint cake and taking photographs, for which purpose Hillary removed his oxygen mask without ill effects. Tenzing produced a string of miscellaneous flags and held them high, while Hillary photographed them. They included the Union Jack, the Nepal flag, and that of the United Nations. Tenzing, who is a devout Buddhist, also laid on the ground in offering some sweets, bars of chocolate, and packets of biscuits.'

He could find himself at times, that Edwardian boy, scraping the barrel of national sporting prestige. Few people could deceive themselves that Britain was originally responsible for the sport of ski-ing, for example. But even there, in this pursuit which the Norwegians had been practising in an organised manner as early as 1767 (when the Norwegian army held ski-races and logged the results), and which Norwegian immigrants had introduced to the British crown colonies of Australia and New Zealand in 1855 and 1857 respectively, and later to America, where miners in the high central ranges skied to work – even there, in this archetypal Scandinavian pursuit, nobody had thought to establish a national or international skiing administration until 1903 when the Ski Club of Great Britain was established by E.C. Richardson. It was followed, almost shamefacedly, by the Ski Associations of Norway and of Sweden, both of which were founded five years later, in 1908.

And as the Edwardian boy grew into manhood he may have observed an amusing but not altogether unusual sight. The British, having got their administrative hands on an entirely alien sport, proceeded to improve upon it. Downhill ski-racing, the version of skiing which would become most popular as a part of the international spectator sport industry, was a British invention – and once again, it had a direct as well as an implicit imperial pedigree. Sir Henry Simpson Lunn, a former Methodist medical missionary to India (and latterly, and more enduringly, a pioneering travel agent) organised the first senior challenge cup for downhill ski-racing in January 1911. It was run over roughly 15 kilometres between a hut close to the 10,000-metre summit of the Wildstrubel and the neighbouring village of Montana in the Swiss Berner Alpèn, and the winner (an Englishman, Cecil Hopkinson) received a trophy presented by one of the greatest soldiers of the Victorian and Edwardian empire, Lord 'Bobs' Roberts of Kandahar.

Eleven years later Henry's son, Arnold Lunn, pioneered the timed slalom ski-run through gates at the Alpine town of Murren, which the family travel agency had by 1922 made famous as a ski resort. In 1930 the international governing body, the Fédération Internationale de Ski, approved the British rules for downhill and slalom racing; in 1931 the Ski Club of Great Britain organised at Murren the first world downhill and slalom ski championships; and in 1936 they became Olympic events.

The Norwegians did not like it. They considered that the British fondness for downhill and slalom skiing stemmed directly from an Anglo-Saxon inferiority. The British, according to the Scandinavians, were too weak to ski effectively across country, and too cowardly to ski-jump. 'What,' a Norwegian plaintively inquired of Arnold Lunn, 'would you think if I changed the rules of cricket?'

'I wish you would,' replied Arnold. 'We might have fewer draws.'

Even the widespread and protean water sports were first corralled and branded by the Victorian British. That elementary activity, swimming, which the Assyrians and Egyptians had clearly enjoyed, became something more than a loose splash about in warm blue water on 7 January 1869 when the representatives of various swimming clubs assembled at the German Gymnasium in London to form the Metropolitan Swimming Association. It immediately held the first National Championship race over one mile on open water in the River Thames (H. Parker won it – swimming, it should be noted, with the then hegemonic breast stroke, for no other was known among white Europeans in 1869 – in 24 minutes 35 seconds). In 1873 its name changed to the Swimming Association of Great Britain.

Meanwhile, the British Abroad were simultaneously at work on this harmless pastime. The first swimming baths had been built in Australia by one Thomas Robinson in 1839 at Woolloomooloo Bay near Sydney; and in 1846 Robinson hosted the first officially recorded swimming races in the antipodes, over 440 yards and 100 yards. By the 1870s swimming was an understandably popular Australian sport, and one Professor Frederick Cavill was offering lessons in keeping afloat at the Lavender Bay Baths in Sydney. Cavill had six sons and three daughters. One of the sons, Dick Cavill, found himself one day in Sydney Bay watching a Solomon Islander named Alick Wickham swimming in a curiously effective manner: Wickham brought his arms up and over his shoulder before reaching down into the water and dragging himself along more quickly and effortlessly than Cavill, with his breast stroke, had ever been able to manage.

Dick Cavill took the stroke back to Lavender Bay Baths, developed it himself, and christened the style which was to revolutionise competitive (and, for that matter, recreational) swimming 'the Australian crawl'. He then, in collaboration with his siblings, worked on a strange double-arm breast stroke which became known as the 'butterfly'. The story of the Cavills had an ending which was almost unique in the annals of imperial sport. In 1905 Dick Cavill did indeed dominate sprint swimming: he held the world record over 100 yards. But the Solomon Islander from whom he had purloined his style, Alick Wickham, was not airbrushed from the record books – Wickham, in that same year, held the record for the 50-yard sprint.

Clear blue water had the potential for more sport than simple swimming. In its first year of existence, 1870, the Metropolitan Swimming Association passed a resolution which proposed 'that a committee be appointed to draw up a set of laws for the game of "football in water"'.

Such a game had, we know, been enjoyed at Leeds (with a rugby ball), and at Burton-on-Trent (with a soft round india-rubber ball, which had to be grounded at one end of the bath despite a goalkeeper who stood on the edge of the pool and was allowed to jump on top of an attacking opposing player). And on 13 July 1876 the Bournemouth Premier Rowing Club staged 'the first series of aquatic handball matches' off the pier. They insisted upon teams of seven-a-side, who competed on a watery field 50 yards long between goals which were marked out by flags. In 1877 the game spread to Scotland, where the Bon Accord Club Gala featured an exhibition match, and by 1884 the Midland Counties Amateur Swimming Association had instituted a national aquatic football championships (which, for the record, were won by the Birmingham and Leander Club).

In 1888 the Amateur Swimming Association, a direct descendant of the Swimming Association of Great Britain, swooped on the new game and imposed a set of official championship rules and a fresh name. The rules specified that a player must be swimming when passing or playing the ball (previously standing had been allowed, which 'displayed unnecessary roughness'). The new name was water polo.

It reached Sydney, Australia, before 1889. The first international water polo match between England and Scotland was played in 1890 (Scotland won). An international board was established in 1892, and in 1900, at the second modern games, water polo became an Olympic sport. The gold medal was won in that year by the Manchester-Osborne Club, which represented Britain. In 1904 it went to the New York Athletic Club, but British teams retained the gold medal in 1908, 1912 and 1920 – by which time water polo had taken hold in central Europe, and the Hungarians were about to launch upon their decades of dominance.

What was there left to organise? One or two things, one or two . . . visitors to Blackpool Tower and St George's Baths, London, in the 1880s and 1890s may have seen young men and women in bathing costumes offering displays of 'Scientific and Ornamental Swimming'. A water polo player named Charlie Smith introduced 'trick swimming' to his Southport club in 1906, and in 1907 the Australian Annette Kellerman toured the USA with an aquatic performance which involved her cavorting gracefully in a large glass water tank. By the 1920s music was being played behind these exhibitions, and the British Abroad in Canada had adopted the entertainment and had hosted amateur championships. In 1943 the Canadians ruled that in full competition, all aspects of this water ballet must be synchronised. The Canadian Amateur Synchronised Swimming Association sub-sequently toured Europe demonstrating the sport . . . and in 1984 synchronised swimming, arguably the strangest of the empire games, became an Olympic event – over, literally, the dead body of the Inter-national Olympic Committee's former chairman, Avery Brundage.

As he put away his sporting annual on that Boxing Day of, shall we say, 1911, our young Edwardian chap could look back with a satisfied sigh upon half a century of neurotic national activity. What games his countrymen had not invented, they had, almost without exception, disciplined. Britain had created a sporting world in the image of its own empire, and for a few brief happy seasons British and colonial athletes as well as administrators would dominate that sporting world.

The blemishes, the faultlines, were not readily apparent in 1911. It would have taken a keen eye to spot them, and such critics were thin on the ground. They were there, of course, and by the end of the twentieth century they would appear as canyons on the historical map. They were there in all of the empire games. They were present in cycling as much as cricket, hockey as well as football. They cut deeply even into the apparently smooth façade of the sport of swimming. Although the Edwardian sporting annual would not have dwelt on such unseemly details, the organisation of imperial swimming had been seriously disrupted for two long years between 1884 and 1886, when nine member clubs of the Swimming Association of Great Britain had resigned from the body over one hugely important issue: an issue which would continue to bedevil and divide the sport for a further two decades.

The issue was a point of principle: of the very highest principle. To many people it had come to be more important than the game itself. It was the philosophy behind imperial sport, the idealism which – as almost all assumed – elevated the British players above all of their predecessors, and guaranteed to the wholesome new world of British sport a future clean and bright and Christian.

The issue, the Holy Grail of the empire games, was amateurism.

CHAPTER SEVEN

Amateurism and the Modern Olympics

> If you intend to embark upon some branch of sport as a career or in order to achieve high amateur championship honours, then without further delay you should find out where there is a good gymnasium.
>
> *The Boy's Book of Sport*, Carlton Wallace, 1951

In a Warwickshire twilight in 1886, a 23-year-old Frenchman experienced an epiphany. 'Alone,' he would later write, 'in a the great Gothic chapel of Rugby, my eyes fixed on the funeral slab on which, without epitaph, the great name of Thomas Arnold was inscribed, I dreamed that I saw before me the cornerstone of the British Empire.'

It was quite a dream. Pierre Fredy, Baron de Coubertin, enjoyed the pure, untroubled conviction of the convert. He did not originate the notion that British greatness stemmed from the games lessons of the country's public schools. The Duke of Wellington was, after all, credited with that line about the Battle of Waterloo having been won on the playing fields of Eton, and the Duke of Wellington had died, aged 83, in 1852. For many a long year before that summer's dusk of 1886 in the chapel of Rugby School, men and women of the British Empire had gladly entertained the notion that their extraordinary national predilection for sport was, in some quasi-mystical manner, linked to their international military and political and trading successes.

Pierre de Coubertin was perfectly placed in time and temperament to swallow whole the mythology that one sprang from the other – that, rather than sport and imperial progress being part of the same expansive phenomenon, the former actually gave birth to the latter. His own country, France, was stagnant and defeatist following the humiliating war with Germany which had begun when he was seven years old and ended one year later, early in 1871, with William I of Prussia donning an imperial crown in, of all places, the Palace of Versailles.

Could such an ignominy have been visited upon Britain? Of course not. Why? Pierre Fredy travelled there to find out. The difference, he determined, lay in education. And the chief difference between British education and that of any other country in the world was its emphasis on games. 'The role played by sport,' he would comment, 'is what appears most worthy of notice in English education.'

He was wrong about many things. He was wrong about Thomas Arnold and Rugby School. The sainted doctor of *Tom Brown's Schooldays*, who was headmaster at Rugby between 1828 and his death in 1842, actually detested sport, and only agreed to its presence on the Rugby curriculum after he had been persuaded that some legitimate controlled physical activity was necessary to divert the boys from burning down the senior common rooms (violent pupil rebellions were commonplace in the public schools of Arnold's time). He was wrong to believe that public-school sports offered a pure code of civilised behaviour to impressionable young men – any sensible reading even of *Tom Brown's Schooldays* suggested that they were just as likely to be useful vehicles for raw-boned bullies to trample upon squealing 12-year-olds. De Coubertin would actually have been more at home with his contemporary, James Edward Cowell Welldon, who was headmaster at Harrow between 1885 and 1898 (before leaving for the bishropric of Calcutta), and who wrote: 'Englishmen are not superior to Frenchmen or Germans in brains or industry, or the science or apparatus of war . . . the pluck, the energy, the perseverance, the good temper, the self control, the discipline, the co-operation, the esprit de corps, which merit success in cricket or football, are the very qualities which win the day in peace or war . . . In the history of the British Empire, it is written that England has owed her sovereignty to her sports.'

But mundane details never bothered visionaries, and Pierre Fredy, Baron de Coubertin, was a visionary. The England of the 1880s and 1890s, the England of J.E.C. Welldon, fed his ideals to the point of surfeit. All around him, on each and every visit, were glittering examples of sports being organised, codified and constituted. Clubs, meets, matches and events sprang out of the soil like autumn mushrooms. And they had, to a single-minded, pure-at-heart observer like de Coubertin, one glorious common thread. They all seemingly aspired to a clean and Christian concept named amateurism.

Amateurism was a hypocritical fraud. Amateurism was written into the legislative body of British sport by the moneyed classes in order to keep out the lower orders. Amateurism was, from its earliest days in the middle of the nineteenth century, nothing more than a crude exclusive device.

The early amateurs were unashamed of that fact, and were not afraid to make it clear. The first athletics clubs that the modern world had seen were established in the south of England in the 1860s (one of them, the Mincing Lane Club, was founded in 1863 and would survive until the close of the twentieth century as the London Athletic Club, the oldest in the world). Before very long the word 'club' would become so familiar to sportsmen and women, so linked to the vocabulary of athletics, that its meaning in the 1860s would subtly change, and the reason why those public schoolboys and university graduates first called themselves the Mincing Lane Club, or the Civil Service Athletic Club (1866), or the Amateur Athletic Club (also 1866) would be forgotten.

It was because clubs were, by definition, exclusive. Clubs were not democratic social institutions. Athletics clubs were not, in the 1860s, bodies designed to deliver sporting amenities to the deprived general public. They were rather self-selecting groups of privileged young men who chose to associate with one another, on the (occasionally thin) pretext of a fondness for running and jumping.

The very last thing that those young men wanted of their clubs was that some barbarous oik should be admitted purely on the grounds that he was good at athletics. In an important sense – and ultimately, in a sense disastrous to British sporting achievement – athletic ability came second as a reason for belonging to a sports club of the second half of the nineteenth century. The company came first. And the company was exclusive.

To the young gentlemen of the mid-nineteenth-century upper classes, the easiest and most obvious way of dissociating themselves and their sporting trophies permanently from the superior working-class runners who raced in Scotland and in the north of England using professional names like racehorses – the Gateshead Clipper, for example, and the North Star – was to exclude men who had ever accepted prize money. Such runners were deliberately excluded not only from the official race meets of the time, but also from the national teams and the record books – out of which they were airbrushed like disfavoured Soviet politicians. So a sprinter such as Arthur Wharton, whose father was a Wesleyan missionary from Grenada and whose mother was the daughter of a Scottish Caribbean trader, could run the 100 yards in 10 seconds at Stamford Bridge in July 1886, at a time when no amateur was capable of achieving the distance in less than 10.5 seconds, and promptly disappear from history. There would never be any mention of Arthur Wharton in the records of the AAA, the log-books of official British athletics. He would die in 1930 after spending the last 15 years of his life working down a Yorkshire coal-mine, and be buried in an unmarked pauper's grave.

Wharton had been a black professional footballer at the time of his astonishing sprinting feats (astonishing because no European would break 10 seconds over 100 metres for a further 100 years), but just to be sure, they also excluded anybody who had ever worked with his hands. So . . . 'An amateur,' read the rules of the Amateur Athletic Club, which was formed by Oxbridge graduates in 1866, 'is a person who has never competed in an open competition, or for public money, or for admission money, and who has never at any period of his life taught or assisted in the pursuit of athletic exercise as a means of livelihood, or is a mechanic, artisan, or labourer.'

'Or is a mechanic, artisan, or labourer . . .' This early definition of sporting amateurism by one of the most influential clubs would come to be seen, in the following century, as alarmingly indiscreet. It was no more than honest. The Victorian amateur athlete was a man (not, of course, a woman) preferably of private means. If private means eluded him he might – and only might – be grudgingly allowed a white-collar job. But mechanics, artisans and labourers should not trouble themselves to apply. The world of amateur athletics was never built for them.

The world of amateur athletics was not even built for shopkeepers. In 1872 the London Athletic Club relaxed its rules slightly, and allowed 'tradesmen' to enter. Sixty of its members resigned in protest, and *The Times* agreed with them, editorialising that 'outsiders, artisans, mechanics and such like troublesome persons can have no place found for them. To keep them out is a thing desirable on every count. The status of the rest seems better assured and more clear from any doubt which might attach to it . . . loud would be the wail over a chased goblet or a pair of silver sculls which a mechanic had been lucky enough to carry off.'

A mechanic would not have needed to be too lucky to carry off a pair of silver sculls from an amateur boat race of the nineteenth century. As an obvious result of aristocratic exclusion, the standards were low. In 1879 the officials of the Henley Regatta – an event which was visited approvingly by Pierre Fredy, Baron de Coubertin – chose to restate their principles. These then read:

> No person shall be considered an amateur oarsman or sculler – 1) Who has ever competed in any open competition for a stake, money or entrance fee; 2) Who has ever competed with or against a professional for any prize; 3) Who has ever taught, pursued, or assisted in the practice of athletics exercises of any kind as a means of gaining a livelihood; 4) Who has been employed in or about boats for money or wages; 5) Who is or ever has been by trade or employment for wages a mechanic, artisan or labourer.

It would have been laughable, were it not for the fact that the people who phrased those constitutions were the same people who were shaping the immediate future of Britain's, and therefore the world's, organised sports. Their desire to exclude from competition all of those who had not been conceived within their own elevated social circle was clearly explained in such statements. It was not only a fear of mixing with the lower orders; it was also a justified apprehension that the lower orders, if once admitted, would prove themselves to be better athletes. So in the case of Henley, an 80-year-old retired Thames waterman ('who has been employed in or about boats') would be necessarily barred from entry. He might, despite his aged bones, carry off a trophy. Given the competition, he probably would.

Nowhere, perhaps, was the true nature of amateurism better defined than in the committee rooms of the Leander Rowing Club at Putney, where in 1878 members decreed that – as at Henley – an amateur oarsman could not be 'employed in or about boats'; but on the other hand 'an Officer of HM's Army, or Navy, or Civil Service' was very welcome.

It became necessary for the Victorian British to elevate this sordid code, if only to justify it to themselves. So amateurism became an ethic. A shamelessly protectionist device was transformed into an ideal. Jesuitical intelligences across the length of the country created for amateurism a new and fictional image. It did not exist, they argued, in order to exclude the lower orders. It was rather heaven-sent to the Victorian world in order to protect the virgin purity of the games which God had ordained that the British should create and rule.

Without amateurism, those games – those clean and gorgeous pursuits which our men had carried like so many flags across the world – would become stained and sullied. People would play them not for the sake of their beauty, but for money. Athletics had to be seen rather like nuns, or teenaged brides. They should not be for sale, and only bad, unworthy men put them on the market stance.

This fresh interpretation of amateurism arrived in just enough time to assuage the late-Victorian conscience, and to be introduced to Pierre Fredy. The Baron de Coubertin – an aristocrat himself – swallowed it happily. He can be forgiven. The same men from whom it issued were also often responsible for the miraculous invention and ordering of international sport, the sport which first attracted de Coubertin's eye. If they said that a high-minded, religious ethic – a dissembling coda so strange that it had to be plausible, for who would bother inventing it? – went hand-in-hand with that sport, how was a simple Frenchman to deny it?

Nor was Pierre de Coubertin to know of the distress and division that had already been caused, by the 1880s and 1890s, within British sport by the crusading application of amateurism. Even the amateur oarsmen were divided. In 1891 the 66-year-old socialist scholar Dr Frederick James Furnivall, who had been an enthusiastic sculler since his youth, founded the National Amateur Rowing Association. This deliberate split away from the Henley-based Amateur Rowing Association was designed to establish a sporting body which did not exclude lower-class oarsmen, only professional oarsmen. Furnivall, a co-founder with John Ruskin of the Working Men's College in London, announced: 'We feel that for a University to send its earnest intellectual men into an East End or other settlement to live with and help working-men with their studies and their sports, while it sends its rowing-men into the ARA to say to those working-men, 'You're labourers; your work renders you unfit to associate and row with us' is a facing-both-ways, an inconsistency and contradiction . . .' (It is certainly pertinent to point out that Furnivall was a famous convert from liberal Christianity to agnosticism, and as such was clearly reluctant to replace one irrational superstition with another.)

The dispute was occasionally vicious. The Amateur Athletic Association, which was formed as a national governing body by three

147

Oxford men in 1880, quickly banned from its own ranks professionals from other sports such as cricket and football. In 1882 it established a fund to help prosecute in courts of law those who contravened its amateur edicts, as a direct result of which several runners were actually sentenced to six months hard labour. In 1887 the Lillie Bridge athletics ground at West Brompton was burned to the ground, supposedly as a reprisal by gamblers and semi-professionals against the AAA. In 1896 and 1897 several leading athletes were banned for life for allegedly receiving appearance money.

Amateurism was without precedent in international sport. The very word 'athlete' derived – as many a university man of the time must have known – from the Greek 'athlein', which means to compete for a prize. Amateurism was, in fact, without precedent in British sport. The notion was unrecognised by the Georgians (who were no strangers to snobbery, but who would have mocked any attempt to remove the spice of gambling from cricket, boxing, or the horses), and as late as the 1820s Oxford and Cambridge colleges were employing Thames watermen in their boat crews – just as in the last quarter of the following century mercenary Americans would be imported to improve their chances of success. Those sports such as cricket and boxing which had been organised before the grand epoch of the second half of the nineteenth century, and which had consequently entered the Victorian era without a single amateur notion in their framework, were obliged quickly to cater for the new orthodoxy. They could not and did not entirely reject the professionalism of their heritage, but rather attempted to cater for the two codes of gentlemen and players simultaneously. They walked into the modern age like Siamese twins, until a more practical generation released them from their unnecessary pain.

Amateurism, the muddled code which was designed by the Victorians to keep control of sport in the right hands, was nonetheless seized upon by Pierre de Coubertin. It added an extra dimension to his vision. It had always seemed a little implausible that British imperial confidence and success should be entirely due to boyhood hours spent in a rugby scrimmage. But if there was something else, if there was a spiritual discipline at play here, if there was a missionary purpose to the whole sporting adventure, a Grail to be sought, then the explanation of its remarkable influence became so much easier.

Pierre de Coubertin moved on from Rugby School and Henley to the whimsical Much Wenlock Olympic Games, a successor to the medieval twilight Cotswold Olympicks, which had been held for 50 years in a Shropshire field. He talked keenly to the chief patron of the Much Wenlock Olympian Society, Dr William Penny Brooks, and he then returned to France to form the Union des Sociétés Françaises des Sports Athlétiques.

And so it was that one November day in 1892, following a bicycle race and a fencing match and the ceremonial opening of a new clubhouse, Baron Pierre de Coubertin made a speech in which he proposed that 'on a basis conforming to modern life, we re-establish a great and magnificent institution, the Olympic Games'.

Four years later, on a cold April day in Athens in 1896, de Coubertin's modern Olympics began. He had initially preferred London as a venue. His proclaimed 'basis conforming to modern life' meant that most sports were played according to British rules, and that the British insistence upon amateurism was written into the Olympic code from the beginning. It would have been pointless to observe that the Greek athletes of antiquity, whose achievements were being honoured by those Athenian games in 1896, would have gazed upon the Victorian amateur conception with blank incomprehension. The British representative of the Amateur Athletic Association who attended de Coubertin's International Athletic Congress in Paris in 1894 to help set the stage for the Olympic revival, had pressed home the amateur imperative. De Coubertin himself would never reject it. Professional athletes, he would insist, could never be rounded characters. They would 'give up their whole existence to one particular sport, grow rich by practising it and thus deprive it of all nobility, and destroy the just equilibrium of man by making the muscles preponderate over the mind'. The fact that some working-class sportsmen and sportswomen, whose muscles were already obliged to preponderate over their minds in dull manual labour, might require financial reward in order to play at all would never enter his aristocratic mind. Amateur the games were, and amateur, for the next 90 years, they would remain.

Perhaps the most surprising thing about the modern Olympic movement was that, however much inspiration it owed to Britain, and however many of its codes and constitutions it copied wholesale from the minute books of British sporting bodies, it was undeniably launched and sustained by non-Britons. In fact it came perilously close to being trumped by a purely imperial idea. In 1891 John Astley

Cooper had proposed a Pan-Britannic Festival to celebrate the culture and sports of Victoria's empire. Astley's idea received a lot of support from the dominions but too little from within Great Britain – where the Amateur Athletics Association in particular was reluctant to mix with such brash company – and by 1894 he had dropped it.

Astley's dream did not die, however. On 16 August 1930, 20,000 spectators crammed into the Civic Stadium in Hamilton, Ontario, Canada. They watched in brilliant sunshine as a lone soldier of the Argyll and Sutherland Highlanders entered the arena holding high a Union Jack. Behind him there followed a dazzling procession of athletes from Newfoundland wearing white blazers, from Bermuda in royal blue, British Guiana in maroon, Australia in green and gold, New Zealand wearing white, South Africa in black and white, Wales in blue, Ireland in green, Scotland in royal blue, England in dark blue, and Canada in red. It was the opening ceremony of the first British Empire Games, which would in 1954 become the British Empire and Commonwealth Games, and in 1970 the British Commonwealth Games. It would in 1990 cast off the final imperial veil to become simply the Commonwealth Games. They were too late, since the collapse of John Astley Cooper's plans in 1894, to challenge the supremacy of the modern Olympics.

The first modern Olympics offered its contestants gymnastics, bicycle races, lawn tennis, fencing, marksmanship, track and field events, swimming, and a 40-kilometre road race from the famous old battle site at Marathon to the Pan-Athenian Stadium. The yachting was cancelled due to bad weather. It was a charming affair. King George I of Greece had all of the 300 competitors to breakfast on the opening day, with the exception of the 14 Americans, who had forgotten that the Greeks still used the Julian calendar and consequently arrived 11 days later. There were no gold medals, only silver and bronze, because Pierre de Coubertin considered that gold smelled too badly of gross reward. Two servants from the British Embassy in Athens attempted to enter for the bicycle race but were told that, as working men, they were not strictly amateurs and therefore did not qualify. At the last minute de Coubertin relented and they were allowed in. The single Italian entrant was less fortunate. He walked to Athens from Milan in order to arrive at a peak of fitness, but he could produce no amateur credentials at the Pan-Athenian Stadium and was debarred from entry.

Towards their close the Games' amateur principle seemed to be in danger. Two hundred and thirty of the 300 entrants were Greek, and no Greek had yet won an event. Sponsors hurried forward to offer a range of prizes to the first Hellenic victor. Free clothing for life and the hand of a merchant's daughter in marriage were advertised. On the morning of 10 April 1896 Spiridion Louis, a village postman from rural Attica, completed that inaugural 40-kilometre race from Marathon in 2 hours 58 minutes 50 seconds to take first place and the silver medal. He rejected all gifts save one: a donkey and a cart which retired with him to his native parish, there to work out their time in, the world was assured, harmonious communal use.

By the time the second Olympics opened in Paris in 1900, the British influence was still stronger. De Coubertin's International Olympic Committee had drawn upon a textbook of British sports: as well as the British codes for lawn tennis and track and field events, suddenly there were codes for golf, rugby union, croquet, water polo, and cricket. Field polo and soccer were announced, but found insufficient takers, and so a single game of soccer in which Upton Park of London beat France 4–0 was offered as a demonstration sport. The third Games went in 1904 to St Louis – and then, in 1908, they arrived in Pierre de Coubertin's spiritual home.

The fourth Olympic Games aroused no little concern in their host city of London. The British were becoming uncomfortably aware that foreign competition had caught up with their games. A cost of civilising Europe through sport, reflected the athletic evangelist Theodore Andrea Cook, was to accept the possibility of defeat by one's pupils. The 1908 Games would have to 'be a serious (I was about to say "a desperate") endeavour on our part against all comers'.

In the long term, of course Cook was right. A nation of 45 million people could not expect to get a thousand million others playing its games – 400 million in the Empire itself, as well as the rest of Europe, Asia and the Americas – and then continue to beat them all, in every contest, into the infinite future. It was a remarkable sign of late-colonial confidence that, in 1908, sporting commentators felt obliged to remind their British readers that their athletic representatives would have to work hard to beat the rest of the world.

They did, and they did. The 1908 Olympics were the last great gasp of British supremacy on the track and on the field. The United Kingdom won 108 medals, 49 of them gold. Far behind in second place the United States of America – whose cartoonists back home had previewed the games by depicting Uncle Sam tweaking the British lion's tail – collected just 46 medals of all descriptions (although most of them were ominously collected from the footraces, where they had few challengers). Britain would never again enjoy such dominance. The UK won the soccer. The UK won all five of the boxing divisions, and all four of the sailing classes, and all four of the rowing events. The UK won five of the six cycling events, the water polo, the tennis, and a hat full of swimming medals.

And the UK won the fulsome – and as it turned out, absolutely timeless – acknowledgement of the chairman of the International Olympic Committee, Baron Pierre de Coubertin. Rising to address a banquet of Olympic officials in London on 24 July 1908, de Coubertin addressed them in French: '*L'important dans ces olympiades,*' he said, '*c'est moins d'y gagner que d'y prendre part . . . L'important dans la vie ce n'est point le triomphe mais le combat.*'

Some of the officials required a translation. 'The important thing,' they were told, 'in these Olympic Games is not winning but taking part . . . The important thing in life is not conquering, but fighting well.' They burst into spontaneous applause.

What was more valuable, British success on the field of play, or this final proof of the pervasive influence of British imperial sporting philosophy? There is no doubt which was more lasting. Even the recalcitrant Americans seemed to have grasped the idea. It was one of their poets, Grantland Rice, who would offer, in a verse titled 'Alumnus Football', the lines:

> For when the One Great Scorer comes
> To write against your name,
> He marks – not that you won or lost –
> But how you played the game.

But the Americans, the Australians, the South Africans, the New Zealanders and the continental Europeans were never truly happy with the creed of amateurism. It was designed to accommodate on the playing field a rigid class system, and the New World did not possess an entrenched class system. It was designed to preserve sport for gentlemen of leisure, and the British Abroad were less sure than the British at Home of the worth and natural supremacy of gentlemen of leisure.

What was more, it slowly dawned upon all but the British that the code was frankly damaging to their athletes. Just four years after the London Olympics, at the Stockholm Games, an American Indian athlete named Jim Thorpe became the first and last man to win both the decathlon and pentathlon events. 'You are the most wonderful athlete in the world,' King Gustav V informed Thorpe. 'Thanks, King,' replied Jim. In the following January it emerged that Thorpe had previously played baseball for $60 a week. Pierre de Coubertin's International Olympic Committee promptly stripped him of both titles, removed his name from the record books, and demanded the return of the two medals. Thorpe died in 1952. Thirty years later, in 1982, the medals were restored to his family.

Tension surfaced in all of the empire games. In 1923 the superb American golfer Walter Hagen was runner-up in the British Open Championships. Throughout the week of the tournament the professional Hagen had been barred from the clubhouse. When the awards ceremony was subsequently held in the same clubhouse Hagen retaliated by boycotting it.

Some in the former colonies expressed their regrets at the demise of amateurism. 'Somehow or other,' a veteran American baseball player wrote as early as 1868, 'they don't play ball nowadays as they used to some eight or ten years ago . . . I mean that they don't play with the same kinds of feelings or for the same objects they used to . . . But it's no use talking like a father to you fellows, you're in for 'biz' now, and have forgotten the time when your club's name stood higher as a fair and square club than it does now.'

Even in Australia, which was more prone than most of the remainder of the world to British influence, by the 1890s professionalism was creeping into the supposedly amateur ranks of Australian Rules football. This was, according to one administrator, disastrous to the sport. T.S. Marshall told a conference of the Victorian Football Association in 1896:

> The game is ostensibly played for exercise and healthful recreation. But in reality there is, to the knowledge of delegates, a percentage in nearly all teams – and the percentage is yearly increasing – of men whose absence from the field would be a benefit, and whose presence is due solely to the fact that their connection with the game affords them facilities for leading idle and worthless lives.
>
> These men are in every way a menace to the sport, and it is on account of their degrading influence that parents who have the moral well-being of their sons at heart find themselves compelled to prohibit them from playing. Exception ought certainly be taken to players who live on the game, and whose language and

demeanour, both on and off the field, are discreditable to themselves and to the clubs in whose ranks they appear. Something
must be done towards weeding such men out.

They weeded themselves out. Shortly after Marshall had finished
speaking a group of Australian Rules clubs broke away to found the
professional Victorian Football League – 'and with it,' wrote the
sports historians Ian Turner and Leonie Sandercock, 'came formal
recognition that football was no longer a game for the pleasure of a
handful of gentleman amateurs but had become an entertainment for
many thousands of predominantly working class supporters, provided
by men who were rewarded in one form or another for their services.'

Of all of the countries whose athletes found themselves burdened
by de Coubertin's insistence upon Olympian amateurism, it was of
course the originator, Britain, which clung most tenaciously to the
principle. Administrators back in the old country would continue to
do so, in Quixotic ignorance of the tide of the twentieth century. As
late as 1956, British athletes travelling to the Melbourne Olympics
found themselves under the wing of the long-serving secretary of the
British Amateur Athletics Board, Jack Crump, who adamantly
refused to issue them with pocket money – a legal loophole in the
amateur legislation which almost every other competing nation was
by then exploiting to help their competitors through an expensive
period. Once in Australia those athletes who had not been to Oxford
or Cambridge universities felt themselves to be snubbed by a
favoured Oxbridge clique. They complained to Crump. 'In general,'
Jack Crump would reflect, 'the less fortunately educated tended to
display a slight inferiority complex and were less ready to feel on
equal terms with the university athletes, as the latter were fully
prepared to accept.'

Amateurism would be a persistent drain on the energy of British
sport throughout the twentieth century. Those games which, like
rugby, were not actually divided into two separate codes because of
amateurism, were almost inevitably weakened by a form of athletic
apartheid which kept the professionals away from their unpaid
colleagues. A group of small islands which was already stretched on
many sporting fronts could not afford such vanity. Some of the best
runners and jumpers, men and women who graced professional
meets at places like Edinburgh's Powderhall Grounds, would never
represent Great Britain in the Olympics. Many of the most qualified
professional cricketers were not permitted to captain – or even to play

for – England. British rugby union lost a steady stream of players to professional rugby league, in a way which was incomprehensible to the shamateurs of the Southern Hemisphere. Golfing club professionals were frequently overlooked when it came to both local and national selection.

And the amateurs who had been bred to play for Britain were, even when they had natural ability, frequently poorly coached by unprofessional part-timers. 'The American athlete,' lamented the Cambridge University blue Philip Noel Baker in 1912, 'specialises in one or two events; before any race of great importance he devotes most of his energies and time to his training; he has a coach – often a professional – who likewise devotes his whole time and energies to his coaching; he has an organisation behind him which is managed by paid organisers – which system depends on organising ability and intelligence, supported by a reasonable amount of money.'

Then, to heap Pelion upon Philip Noel Baker's Ossa, along came communism.

There was a delicious irony in the western amateur sports administrator's hostile attitude towards the 'state amateurs' of the communist countries. On the face of it, they were playing by the book. Communism did not reward its sportsmen and women over other citizens. Communist governments were just as opposed in their own ideologies to grossly rich professional athletes, as they were opposed to grossly rich farmers or industrialists. Communism, travelling down a different road, had thereby rediscovered the virtues of amateurism. The communist athlete was typically a soldier, or a civil servant, or a games teacher who was found a job which complemented his or her sporting ambitions, much as British rugby union players in their last years of amateurism were often placed in semi-sinecures by sympathetic commercial companies. Communism reinvented amateurism for the commoner.

This was disturbing to the high priests of amateurism in the English-speaking world. It was slightly worrying because godless communism could not possibly be regarded as doing anything right; but mostly because the communists had missed the point, they had got the idea all wrong. Amateurism was not designed for games teachers with time on their hands and facilities within their reach: amateurism was designed for gentlemen of leisure who did not have to work at all, let alone run in races. If working people achieved anything in amateur sport, they had traditionally to do so only after massive sacrifices and gruelling preparations. They had to put in their nine-hour day at the mill or the office before running their 15 miles through the nights of a Pennine winter. Then, and then only, would they receive the enormous condescension of such as Jack Crump. Anything else – any suggestion of the Grail of amateurism being made easily available to all of the population – was simply taking unfair advantage of the technical definition of amateurism. What chance would the true Oxbridge amateur aristocrat have against 200 million well-trained Soviets? The communists may have found themselves within the strict rules of the International Olympic Committee, but the whole boiling smacked of sharp practice, of cheating, and the British were not afraid to say so. Those gold medals which began routinely to find their way back to Russia, East Germany, Hungary and Romania in the 1950s and 1960s were somehow, in the eyes of the British amateur establishment, tarnished. They were intended, after all, for men of property and breeding; men who had been 'fortunately educated'. If the Russians had managed to dispossess or shoot all of that class, it would arguably be better for all concerned if they kept out of athletics altogether.

The middle of the twentieth century was not a comfortable period for the British amateur sporting imperialist. On the one hand the Soviets were exploiting the old credo to swamp international games meets with wonderfully talented and perfectly trained Red Army sergeants of both sexes. On the other hand, it did not do to examine too closely the Nazi devotion to old-fashioned amateurism. That was plainly embarrassing. It had been something – yet another thing – to admire about pre-war Germany, but by the later 1940s it was better forgotten. One tried not to reflect, as one mused over the recent histories of the games which Britain had offered to the world, on the fate of rugby league football in occupied France. In 1939 it had been a strong and popular sport, particularly in the south-west of the country. The Vichy government which ruled southern France after the German conquest of 1940 decided that professional sport had contributed to the failure of the nation. They established a government department under the Wimbledon tennis champion Jean Borotra, whose brief was to make all French sports, from soccer to cycling, amateur. Borotra and his colleagues decided instantly that rugby league was nothing more than a professional version of rugby union football. The funds of the French Rugby League were confiscated by the Vichy state, and its players were instructed to play rugby union.

The action taken by the regime of Marshal Pétain may have been uncommonly drastic, but it was difficult to avoid the realisation that it had reached almost precisely the same conclusions as had its countryman, Pierre Fredy, in the chapel of Rugby School 54 years earlier.

CHAPTER EIGHT

Cricket: The Ultimate Imperial Sport

> There is no game in the world more sporting than cricket. The
> word itself is used in everyday conversation to express the idea of
> fair play. 'It's not cricket,' we say, when we want to object to
> something that is unfair.
>
> *The Boy's Book of Sport*, Carlton Wallace, 1951

In the middle of the 1870s the English naturalist Henry Nottidge
Moseley, an Old Harrovian and an Oxford man, was searching for
platypus in the region of Coranderrk in Victoria, Australia. He could
not persuade a single 'incorrigibly lazy' aborigine to find him a
platypus, however. Instead they took him to a bush cricket match . . .

'We found the cricket party,' Moseley would report, 'in high
spirits, shouting with laughter, rows of spectators being seated on logs
and chaffing the players with all the old English sallies: 'Well hit!',
'Run it out!', 'Butter fingers!' etc . . . The men were all dressed as
Europeans; they knew all about Mr W.G. Grace and the All-England
Eleven . . .'

Early in the following century a member of the Indian Police
Service named H.T. Wickham found himself stationed in Kashmir.
While there he was regularly drawn to a cricket match which was
organised by a local potentate. The sides would be selected and play
would commence in the usual fashion. And then:

> At three o'clock in the afternoon that Maharajah himself would
> come down to the ground, the band would play the Kashmir
> anthem, salaams were made, and he then went off to a special tent
> where he sat for a time, smoking his long water pipe.

158

At four thirty or thereabouts he decided he would bat. It didn't matter which side was batting, his own team or ours. He was padded by two attendants and gloved by two more, somebody carried his bat and he walked to the wicket looking very dignified, very small and with an enormous turban on his head. In one of the matches I happened to be bowling and my first ball hit his stumps, but the wicket keeper, quick as lightning, shouted 'No Ball' and the match went on. The only way that the Maharajah could get out was by lbw. And after fifteen or twenty minutes batting he said he felt tired and he was duly given out lbw. What the scorers did about his innings, which was never less than half a century, goodness only knows.

Seventy years after that, in the summer of 1981 Geoffrey Watkins found himself describing for *The Times* a game of cricket featuring both men and women in Apia, the capital of Western Samoa.

The concrete wicket is slightly longer than ours and four feet wide. It is raised about three inches off the ground so this makes no-balling virtually impossible. The bats are three-sided and 44 inches long, tapering to a rounded handle bound in coconut cord. Individual marks in bright colours are painted on the base part . . . There are no bails as the strong sea breezes would keep shipping them off.

The teams are 20-a-side and it is a picturesque sight when they take the field in their colourful lavalavas (cotton wraparound skirts worn by both sexes), wearing T-shirts and bare-footed. Each side brings its own umpire . . . The batting side does not repair to the pavilion when the game begins as there is no such place. Instead the other 18 players sit in a semicircle in the position of the slips. Most of the fielders being on the leg side as the game proceeds – runs are called points – the seated batting side will break into song: sad traditional melodies or war chants accompanied by handclapping . . .

The batsmen have two stances. Some will rest the bat over their shoulder as if waiting to brain some creature emerging from the swamps, while others point it to the ground like a golfer lining up for a prodigious drive; and both men and women, perhaps a little inelegantly, thrust the folds of their lavalavas between their muscular thighs before taking guard.

All the bowlers are fast and they only take three or four paces before hurling the ball down. Women bowl underarm. The ball is always well pitched up, usually middle and leg, and rises sharply. Sometimes the batsmen were hit in the tenderest of places. As they scorn such sissy aids as helmets, boxes, gloves and pads, I winced for them. But they seemed unaffected and just laughed when they were hit.

In fact, whatever the players did they laughed in doing it: dropping a catch, being out first ball, missing a run-out or whatever were causes for loud laughter, and they laughed just as loudly when making a mighty hit into the sun or into the long grass in the outfield where fielders were up to their waist in couch grass.

Cricket was quintessentially the imperial sport. In the course of Queen Victoria's reign, it progressed from being the game which no foreigner – in particular, no continental European – could or should attempt to learn, to being the game which the British Abroad were best advised to carry with them and to introduce to their new indigenous charges. For cricket could make them understand.

There was something fittingly oriental about cricket's elevation to a serpentine ritual, something which reflected the contemporaneous British yearning for the wonder and magic of the east. The bat, the ball and the wicket, it was seriously suggested, constituted a form of Trinity. Hours spent under their influence could somehow affect the character, just as a later generation would believe that razor blades left inside a miniature pyramid would never blunt. This was the faith which found its most famous expression in Henry Newbolt's poem 'Vitaï Lampada' ('Torches of Life'). Newbolt switched effortlessly from the tense finish in bad light of a school cricket match, in which a captain's exhortation to his last inexperienced batsman helps him to face the final hour's play, to a military disaster in a desert campaign at which the only proof of hope is that same young cricketer's piping repetition of his school's cricket captain's words:

> This they all with a joyful mind
> Bear through life like a torch in flame,
> And falling fling to the host behind –
> 'Play up! play up! and play the game!'

There is no word of victory, or even of a draw successfully accomplished on Newbolt's cricket pitch, and – probably sensibly, given the British record in desert campaigns – no implication that his battle was saved. If anybody survived, Newbolt suggests, they survived with pride only because of the young cricketer's honour. If, as seemed likely, he died, he died well, and the host which followed him seized his torch, and at the end of the day that was all that mattered.

No other sport could deliver this resonant message. Rugby was fun, tennis a jape, and association football could be positively dangerous. Soccer was the antithesis of cricket. Sir Robert Baden-Powell, the hero of Mafeking and founder of the Boy Scout movement, felt himself obliged to warn that this burgeoning spectator sport, 'football . . . is a vicious game when it draws crowds of lads away from playing the game themselves to be merely onlookers at a few paid performers . . . Thousands of boys and young men, pale, narrow-chested, hunched up, miserable specimens, smoking endless cigarettes, numbers of them betting, all of them learning to be hysterical as they groan and cheer in panic in unison with their neighbours.'

In the starkest of contrasts, as Baden-Powell's contemporary Lord George Harris would have it, cricket was 'more free from anything sordid, anything dishonourable, than any game in the world. To play it keenly, honourably, generously, self-sacrificingly is a moral lesson in itself, and the classroom is God's air and sunshine.'

The Victorian British did not introduce cricket to their Empire solely because they enjoyed the game. They took it with them because they felt that they had a duty to do so. Just as it taught discipline and honour to their own young officer cadets, so those qualities might rub off on to some of the subject peoples. Just as it delivered a moral lesson to Englishmen, so it might have a missionary effect upon Asians, native Australians and Polynesian islanders.

It was a curious transformation of a rude old sport. Back in the eighteenth century, when cricket still advertised its Celtic origins by its use of a curved bat, the game was sparsely played in both town and country: so, far from being a national cultural icon, it was not even a major popular recreation like football, or bando. The first identifiable realisation of the English cricketing fantasy arrived in 1833, when a London publisher and erstwhile friend of John Keats named Charles Cowden Clarke collected, edited and issued the sporting memories of a Hampshire man named John Nyren. Nyren had played cricket with a group of friends in the vale of Hambledon at the end of the eighteenth century, and his collected reminiscences (titled *The Young Cricketer's Tutor*) proved to be absolutely seminal. Not only did they establish in the popular English consciousness an image of this lush Hampshire vale as the birthplace of cricket; but also they delivered, five years before the accession of Queen Victoria, a sense of cricket as a virtuous activity and of cricketers as decent Englishmen. Nyren's men were steadfast and true, resolute and just, democratic by instinct, shy by preference and slow to condemn but – one always understood – potentially terrible in their righteous anger.

The influence of *The Young Cricketer's Tutor* is impossible to overstate. It delivered a delusory self-portrait to a sport which would become the moral and behavioural touchstone of the rulers of half the world. For a century and a half after its publication, Clarke's book on Nyren echoed throughout England, and its reverberations could be distantly heard in the farthest corners of the earth.

John Nyren's batsman/wicket-keeper, for example, was named Tom Sueter.

> He had an eye like an eagle – rapid and comprehensive. He was the first who departed from the custom of the old players who deemed it a heresy to leave the crease for the ball; he would get in at it and hit it straight off and straight on; and, egad! it went as if it had been fired . . .
>
> It was as if, too, Mother Nature wanted to show at his birth a specimen of her prodigality, she gave him so amiable a disposition that he was the pet of all the neighbourhood; so honourable a heart that his word was never questioned by the gentlemen associated with him; and a voice which for sweetness, power, and purity of tone (a tenor) would with proper cultivation have made him a handsome fortune. With what rapture have I hung upon his notes when he has given us a hunting-song in the club-room after the day's practice was over.

One hundred and ten years after the publication of *The Young Cricketer's Tutor* (and 150 years after the era which it purported to describe), the poet and biographer Edmund Blunden chose a time of grave national crisis, the year 1943, to remind Englishmen of who they were. He published in that fourth summer of the Second World

War a book titled *Cricket Country*. It included a profile of another batsman/wicket-keeper, a village parson this time.

> He was well known in many a cricket field besides our own, and in higher company than our local matches attracted; sometimes, it may be, he put over an old sermon because the week's demands on him and his cricket bag had given no time for writing a new one . . .
>
> 'The vicar was a wicket-keeper of heavy build but [with] a light and menacing rapidity in action. As has been hinted, he did not spare the foolish, and they say he played some tricks on his slower-thinking adversaries. I saw him once stump a batsman with such utter speed and indolence mixed as Ames of Kent in later days could show when Freeman lured the striker out of his ground – but the vicar's chance on the occasion I noted was the briefest imaginable. When his turn came to swing the bat he attacked the ball with a vengeance other than the Lord's, but possibly a theologian could explicate a relationship and justify the vicar's own Article. A slovenly bad ball, 'a godly and wholesome doctrine' of driving it and all such out of the earth.

Nothing could be slid between those two men. The tone of them was identical. Across the busiest years in British history, they tip a hat to one another. That was the semi-mythological game and those were the heroic players – unchanged in their own minds' eyes throughout the whole 150-year span of empire – which Britain took to Coranderrk and Kashmir. It should not be assumed that the enthusiastic adoption of the rite guaranteed indigenous people immunity from the excesses of empire. Money and religion always came first. Just 20 years after Henry Nottidge Moseley's delighted visit to that Victorian bush cricket match, the aboriginal community at Coranderrk was violently dispossessed of its land and dispersed. Imperial sport was never intended to serve the local purpose; it was a possession and a function of the colonialists, to be granted or removed at their will. The goalposts, so to speak, could always be shifted.

The Kashmiri Maharajah came closer than the native Australians – closer, even, than he probably suspected – to capturing an essence of old English cricket. The squire on his Sussex meadow would not expect to do much more fielding or fast bowling than would the Indian princeling. He saw himself as a batsman, as a dismissive striker of the slovenly ball. The village blacksmith and the farmhand could wear themselves out hurling down deliveries or scampering about the outfield. Theirs was a strenuous playing life, and a short one. The aristocracy expected to be in suitable shape for lunch.

There never was a truly democratic tradition of cricket in England, where lord and commoner met on a level playing field and the appeal of one was weighed as equally as the appeal of the other. Cricket was organised long before the mid-Victorian ascendancy of amateurism, and it consequently had no history of exclusion: working men played the game, and often shared a wicket with the aristocracy, and both classes saw nothing wrong with turning a penny from the game: the former through appearance fees and the latter from gambling. But their roles and ambitions were distinct and clearly defined. Writing 150 years later of a cricket match which had taken place between Kent and All England in 1746, the historian George Macaulay Trevelyan made a famous claim. 'Squire, farmer, blacksmith and labourer,' he said, 'with their women and children come to see the fun, were more at ease together and happy all the summer afternoon. If the French noblesse had been capable of playing cricket with their peasants, their chateaux would never have been burnt.'

The missed point of Trevelyan's rosy view was that even he found himself surprised by the fact that, for one day in a year in the 1740s, 'noblemen, gentlemen and clergy are making butchers, cobblers or tinkers their companions'. He saw fit to comment on it because it was unusual. He did not see fit to say how far the companionship developed when stumps had been drawn, and he steered clear of the subtle nuances of cricket as a team game which easily, far more easily than any other sport, accommodated class differences during the contest itself. The slip fielder and the stroke-playing batsman might never, in the course of a game, rub shoulders with the bowler and the long on.

There were always gentlemen, and there were always players. By 1842, when Kent once more played All England, the official teamsheet read: 'Kent – Gentlemen, Mr N. Felix, Mr W.D.C. Baker, Mr C.G. Whitaker, Mr W. Mynn, and Mr A. Mynn. Players – Pilch, Wenman, Adams, Dorrington, Hillyer, and Cocker.' Those distinctions would be observed in the teamsheets of English county cricket until 1963. Before 1926 the gentlemen and the players of England used different gates to enter the field. Before 1939 most county clubs had different dressing-rooms for the two classes, and all county captains were amateurs. Not until 1952 did a professional – Len Hutton – captain England, and not until 1962 would *The Times* publish a letter from a professional on the subject of cricket. The difference between cricket and rugby was simply that the professional players and the amateur gentlemen did at least in cricket continue to play the same game. The difference between cricket and athletics was that the cricketing professionals were permitted to perform on the same stage as the amateurs, and to represent their county and their country. 'I say gentlemen were gentlemen,' one of those Kentish players of 1842, Fuller Pilch, would recall in his old age, 'and players were players, much in the same position as a nobleman and his head gamekeeper might be, and we knew our place and they knew theirs.'

In exporting cricket to their colonies the British (and it was the British, for many a Scottish, Welsh or Irish youth of the appropriate class learned the game at Eton or Harrow) were consciously exporting not only a moral lesson in God's classroom, but also a study in deference which was so subtle that it was almost subliminal. Those who did not recognise this fact were none the wiser; those who knew of it, by and large wholeheartedly approved.

Cricket may have been more valuable as an imperial asset than even its most fervent apologists realised. In 1911 as a boy of ten years old the future Marxist and Pan-African nationalist C.L.R. James won a scholarship to the Queen's Royal College in Trinidad. He described his classmates:

> We were a motley crew. The children of some white officials and white business men, middle-class blacks and mulattos, Chinese boys, some of whose parents still spoke broken English, Indian boys, some of whose parents could speak no English at all, and some poor black boys who had won exhibitions or whose parents had starved and toiled on plots of agricultural land and were spending their hard-earned money on giving the eldest boy an education.
>
> Yet rapidly we learned to obey the umpire's decision without question, however irrational it was. We learned to play with the team, which meant subordinating your personal inclinations, and even interests, to the good of the whole. We kept a stiff upper lip in that we did not complain about ill-fortune. We did not denounce failures, but 'Well tried' or 'Hard luck' came easily to our lips. We were generous to opponents and congratulated them

on victories, even when we knew they did not deserve it. We lived in two worlds. Inside the classrooms the heterogeneous jumble of Trinidad was battered and jostled and shaken down into some sort of order. On the playing field we did what ought to be done. Every individual did not observe every rule. But the majority of the boys did. The best and most-respected boys were precisely the ones who always kept them. When a boy broke them he knew what he had done and, with the cruelty and intolerance of youth, from all sides our denunciations poured in on him. Eton or Harrow had nothing on us . . .

I knew what was done and what was not done. One day when I bowled three maiden overs in succession and a boy fresh from England said to me, 'James, you must take yourself off now, three maiden overs,' I was disturbed. I had not heard that one before, this boy was from England and so he probably knew.

A deeply instilled sense of fair play and obedience to the perceived moral codes of a distant land were not, however, the only causes of cricket's extraordinary success in most of the colonies. They would not have been enough to retain the lifelong affection of such as C.L.R. James. They did not explain the adoption of the game of cricket by the Greek islanders of Corfu. There, during the British protectorate of the Ionian Septinsular Union between 1815 and 1864, a cricket pitch was laid out on the esplanade of Corfu Town. At the end of the twentieth century two local teams were still playing on it, having evolved a metrical scoring system (five runs were awarded for a clean boundary, rather than six) and a style of slow bowling which was perfectly adapted to the Mediterranean wicket. The cricketing Corfiotes occasionally and unsuccessfully petitioned their disinterested compatriots at the Athenian state television station for broadcast coverage of international test matches.

Long after the British had withdrawn from such possessions, when British imperial values had become the objects of scorn or absolute hatred, cricket continued to thrive in India, Pakistan and Sri Lanka. Stripped of its colonial pretensions, the game came to be loved for its own sake. It was a complicated sport, arguably the most difficult of all of the empire games to understand, and that may explain why only those nations which had been given free demonstrations by the occupying forces for a minimum of two generations would hold with cricket once the last viceroy had left. But it had been elegantly refined. By the 1780s, when the modern game was ratified, cricket had become an exquisite exercise in delayed gratification. Unlike many others it was a physically democratic game: a good player could lack height, or weight, or speed, or all three. It demanded mental as well as corporeal ability, and it could elicit grace from its performers. Indian princes and English squires may have once been attracted to cricket because, in the words of the Australian historian Richard Cashman, it provided them 'with an outlet for intrigue, pomp and selfish ambition, and for conspicuous consumption'; British colonialists may have carried cricket before them as – with the English language and Christianity – one of the three great imperial totems; but cricket became a massive spectator and participant sport in the old dominions because of the singular and entirely praiseworthy fact that it was a beautiful invention which, in Asian and West Indian hands, became more radiant than ever.

It became, in fact, more popular as well as more attractive in the former colonies than at home. The record crowd for a day at Lord's cricket ground, the ancestral home of that iconic imperial institution the Marylebone Cricket Club, was 33,800 to see England play Australia on 25 June 1933. (In that same decade Hampden Park football stadium in Glasgow attracted 135,000 to several soccer matches.) In India, 70,000 once turned up to see one day of a women's cricket match at Patna and few male Test matches were played before less than 80,000 people. The Sydney cricket ground in Australia accommodated and was regularly filled by 78,000 spectators until the reduction of its capacity in the 1960s. (Only in North America, where it was widely played in colonial times and where teams existed, as we have seen, into the early years of the twentieth century, did cricket fail to expand. It was smothered there, like most other team games which were codified in Britain, by the independent Americans' idiosyncratic adaptation of other European sports.)

And a greater percentage of the population played cricket in the colonies than in Britain. For cricket, while it may have been the emblematic sport of the British Empire, was never the national game of Great Britain, but it would become the national game of the West Indies, Australia and the entire Indian sub-continent. In the place of its birth, it was a snooty child, often reluctant to share its bat with poorer peers, desperate for attention but frequently neglected at school and at home amid a ruck of noisy siblings.

It did not help cricket's cause that the place of its birth was also the breeding ground of a more seductive and accessible game, a sport which would become the most popular and widespread physical recreation in the history of the world — another team ball-game which scrambled out of the brawl of medieval England, and transformed itself into an international obsession.

CHAPTER NINE

Football: An International Obsession

Let into a wall at Rugby School is a granite plaque on which is carved the inscription:

'This stone commemorates the exploit of William Webb Ellis who, with a fine disregard for the rules of Football as played in his time, first took the ball in his arms and ran with it, thus originating the distinctive feature of the Rugby Game. AD 1823.' In those days, if a player caught a football in his arms he had to retire towards his own goal . . . Ellis's strange action seemed to be a new and attractive way of playing football, and rules were soon devised which made it lawful to carry a ball forward during the course of play.

The Boy's Book of Sport, Carlton Wallace, 1951

With the obvious exceptions of the Scottish Presbyterian Church and the Trotskyist left, it is doubtful whether any other British cultural conception has splintered into so many different disciplines as has the simple game of football.

It started with one big and commonplace idea. In the twelfth century that same William FitzStephen who observed the sport of ice-skating in London also noted that:

After dinner all the youth of the City goes out into the fields for the very popular game of ball. The scholars of each school have their own ball, and almost all the workers of each trade have theirs also in their hands. The elders, the fathers, and the men of wealth come on horseback to view the contests of their juniors, and in their fashion sport with the young men; and there seems to be aroused in these elders a stirring of natural heat by viewing so much activity and by participation in the joys of unrestrained youth.

The Victorians were aware of this sport's antiquity. Writing in 1887 the celebrated judge and athlete Sir Montague Shearman stated that:

> The game of football is undoubtedly the oldest of all the English national sports. For at least six centuries the people have loved the rush and struggle of the rude and manly game, and Kings with their edicts, Divines with their sermons, scholars with their cultured scorn and wits with their ridicule have failed to keep the people away from the pastime they enjoyed. Football flourished for centuries before the arts of boating and cricketing were known, and may fairly claim to be not only the oldest but the most essentially popular sport of England.

Such a game was not confined to the British Isles, as the more scholarly Victorians knew. The ancient Spartans had played a sport which they knew as 'episkyros', which involved groups of youths dividing into two teams to force a ball over opposing boundaries. The Romans played a similar game which they knew as 'harpastum', and which they may or may not have introduced to Britain. In northern China a ball game was played which disallowed the use of arms, and by the tenth century AD this had been adopted by the Japanese, re-christened 'kemari' and refined into a ritualistic test of skill: eight players stood in twos at the four corners of a square pitch. One of them first kicked a leather ball into the air three times, and then passed to the next player, who repeated the exercise. The object was to prevent the ball from touching the ground. Soccer players would recognise a form of keepie-uppie. (Although not all soccer players could match the Japanese proficiency: a kemari record of the year 1208 reported that 'kicking has been done 980 times and then 2,000-odd times. The ball was as if hung from the sky without any fall to the ground.')

But for all of the usual reasons, Chinese and Japanese ball-games did not evolve into five or six internationally recognised sports, whereas the crude old British village game of football did. And crude it was. The setting of hundreds of men from neighbouring hamlets (or from different parts of the same town, which occurred at Derby and subsequently left the name of that municipality in the English language as an ordinary noun meaning any sporting contest between proximate people) against each other in a feverish unregulated contest to propel an inflated pig's bladder over an agreed boundary line, would remain part of British popular folklore. It was the south and east's equivalent to the great bando contests of western Wales, or the inter-district shinty matches of the north of Scotland, or the hurling competitions of Cornwall and Ireland.

To many, throughout the ages, it was a truly shocking exhibition. People occasionally died at football festivals, and serious injury was commonplace. The Puritan phamphleteer Philip Stubbes wrote in his *Anatomie of Abuses in the Realme of England* in 1583: 'As concerning football playing I protest unto you that it may rather be called a bloody and murthering practice than a fellowlye sport or pastime. For dooth not everyone lye in waight for his adversarie, seeking to over throwe him and picke him on his nose, though it be on hard stones, on ditch or dale, valley or hill, or whatever place soever it be he careth not, so he have him downe; and he that can serve the most of this fashion he is counted the only felow, and who but he?'

This was the game, uncodified and unlegislated, which in the first half of the nineteenth century found favour on the playing fields of the public schools and of Oxford and Cambridge universities. It was a running maul which took place on a demarcated rectangle between two sets of goalposts. Hands, feet, or any other part of the body could be employed to control and impel the ball. (Although regional variations naturally occurred: some districts, such as Derbyshire and the Scottish borders, seem to have favoured more carrying and throwing than did, for example, Rugby School before the auspicious year of 1823.) Referees, where they existed, concerned themselves with little other than awarding goals and deciding if the ball was still in play. There was effectively no such thing as a foul. 'Hacking', or kicking other players whether or not the ball was in the vicinity, was universally legitimate. ('Hack,' defined the *Oxford English Dictionary*, '= cut with rough blows, notch, mangle; kick shin of [opponent at football] . . .') Hacking was in fact regarded by many as an essential ingredient of this manly exercise. As a former player in the school magazine *New Rugbeian* fondly reminisced in 1860:

> Fellows did not give a fig for the ball except in as much as it gave
> them a decent pretext for hacking. I remember a scrummage
> down by the touchline near the pavilion. By Jove! that was some-

thing like a scrummage! Why, we'd been hacking for five minutes already and hadn't had half enough. Take my word for it, all you youngsters, if you just watch a fellow of the old school playing, and take a leaf out of his book, you'll get on a long sight better than if you take up any of the fiddle faddle of the present day. My maxim is – hack the ball when you see it near you, and when you don't, why then hack the player next to you . . . Dash my buttons! you haven't a chance of getting a decent fall in the present day; and no wonder either when you see young dandies 'got up regardless of expense', mincing across Big Side, and looking just as if their delicate frames wouldn't survive any violent contact with the ball. Hang the young puppies! We shall have fellows playing in dress boots and lavender-coloured kid gloves before long.

There actually was a pupil named William Webb Ellis, who attended Rugby School between 1816 and 1825. The famous plaque commemorating the boy who impudently 'first took the ball in his arms and ran with it, thus originating the distinctive feature of the rugby game' in 1823 was not itself erected until 1895, however, and Ellis remains a shadowy figure with an almost apocryphal biography. He went up to Oxford from Rugby, and there he won a cricket blue. For 17 years he was rector at the village of Magdalen Laver near Harlow in Essex, but he contrived to be buried at Menton on the French Riviera, where his gravestone was discovered in 1959 by the latter-day imperialist and sportswriter Ross McWhirter (who himself met an imperial death: he was killed by the Irish Republican Army in 1975 for sponsoring an award scheme designed to capture IRA terrorists).

What remains of Ellis other than the plaque and an undeserved reputation as the sole originator of rugby football are a couple of memories. In 1880 one of his contemporaries at Rugby, a solicitor and antiquary called Matthew Holbeche Bloxam, recalled that in a game towards the end of 1823 Ellis had contravened the Rugby School football tradition. He had caught the ball, and then instead of dutifully returning it to the opposition and retreating to await a further attack he had run goalwards with it in his hands. 'I remember William Webb Ellis perfectly,' recollected another old school chum, the Reverend Thomas Harris, in 1897. 'He was generally inclined to take unfair advantage at football.'

That was the ill-defined sport which, in 1846, a group of under-

graduates at Cambridge University attempted to thrash into ord
They were motivated partly by a desire to outlaw handling, and
extirpate hacking. Hacking was not, despite the published views or
Rugbeian old boys, universally popular. 'Today's the School-house
match,' wrote one such old boy, Thomas Hughes, in *Tom Brown's
Schooldays*. 'Our house plays the whole of the school at football. And
we all wear white trousers, to show'em we don't care for hacks.' In
the muscular Christian perspective, hacking was more likely to be the
province of such as the immortal school bully, Harry Flashman.

The Cambridge rules, then, formed the basis for the rules of the
Football Association, which was established at a meeting at the
Freemason's Tavern in London's Lincolns Inn Fields in October
1863. From the word 'association' came an affectionate diminutive:
'I'm going to play a little rugger,' one public school sportsman of the
time would winsomely declare, 'then perhaps a little crikker, and on
Saturday it's soccer.'

One of the clubs at that inaugural meeting, Blackheath, became
unhappy with the results, and many others which had not attended
were reluctant to sacrifice their local traditions to homogeneity. So
Harrow and Rugby retained both handling and hacking, and in
collaboration with Blackheath the public schools formed a Rugby
Football Union in 1871. It, too, to the horror of many of the
members, promptly abandoned hacking.

But the games were from that year onward distinct; identifiably
separate versions of football; one a handling sport and the other a
game which disallowed use of the hands in all but the goalkeeper.
They were also distinct in other ways. The patrimony of rugby union
meant that it retained the stronger support in the public schools and
at the universities (even in Scotland: when the first international
match was played in 1871 between Scotland and England, two
universities and three public schools provided the bulk of the Scottish
players), while soccer found a new constituency elsewhere. The
latter, soccer, would as a result become a populist sport, one which
spread most thoroughly among the labouring masses of the world.
But the former, rugby union, would become more consciously an
imperial game, one which was imposed from above for the good of
its participants.

They both travelled to North America. By the 1860s Harvard and
Yale universities played rugby-style and soccer-style football respectively. In 1876 Yale agreed to adapt to Harvard's handling game, and
by the late 1880s the American colleges had introduced many of the

differences – blocking, alternating ball possession, fixed number of downs – which would in turn differentiate American football from rugby.

They travelled to Ireland, where rugby football was codified as a separate game called Gaelic football. They also experienced parallel evolution in Australia. There a curious hybrid of the two codes became known as Australian Rules football. Football of the unspecified kind had probably been played in newly colonised Australia since the end of the eighteenth century (and certainly since 1829, when Irish soldiers were reported as playing a game in Sydney). In 1858 an organised game was played between the schoolboys of Scotch College and Melbourne Grammar. That game was refereed by one Thomas Wentworth Wills, a former schoolteacher at Rugby. Wills promoted the game of his old school to the point that in May 1859 a meeting was held in Melbourne to codify the sport.

At that time, of course, neither soccer nor rugger had themselves been properly nationally codified and administrated in Britain. So an ad hoc committee found itself drawing up rules for an entirely fresh sport. Unlike the Football Association and the Rugby Union, they did not outlaw fully half of the aspects of the old game; instead they created a recreation which embraced many of the old school codes. Victorian Rules football, or Melbourne Rules, as it was known until the 1880s, allowed handling and kicking – but not hacking, which was instantly outlawed in 1859. Throwing was at first banned, which led to the idiosyncratic Australian Rules technique of holding the ball in one hand and punching it with the closed fist of the other. Goals were to be scored in soccer fashion: by kicking the ball rather than carrying it over the line.

The odd and certainly unintentional result of all of this was that, at the end of the twentieth century, anybody wishing to see a cleaned-up approximation of the British game from which sprang rugby football, association football, American football and Gaelic football, could do no better than to witness an Australian Rules football match.

But Australia was the exception. It organised its own codified version of primitive football before the same was done in Britain, and that was an extremely unusual occurrence. Rugby union and rugby league – and even soccer – would later arrive there, and the first two would achieve considerable success in the antipodes, but they could not and would not dominate the handling game there. That 1859 meeting in Melbourne made sure of that.

Elsewhere rugby was delivered to the colonies as the finished item. Charles Munro, the son of a New Zealand politician, was sent for his education to Sherbourne School in England, and when he returned to the southern seas in 1870 he persuaded his town club at Nelson, which had hitherto been toying with Australian Rules, to try rugby union. They did, and the road to the All Blacks was open. At the same time in South Africa an alumnus of Winchester College, Canon Ogilvie, suggested to the young men of Cape Town that rugby union might provide a 'healthy form of winter exercise'.

And peculiarly among the more imperial of British sports, it even made its way to the European continent. British students played rugby in Le Havre in the 1870s, to the apparent amusement of the locals. By 1892, however, there were 20 French rugby clubs and a club championship was launched. The 1920 Olympics as the venue of an extraordinary sight: a rugby union Olympic competition for which only two sides entered, France and the United States of America. Even more unexpectedly, the Americans won. Four years later, in 1924, the Olympics returned to Paris. Thirty thousand people turned up to see Gallic revenge when France met the USA in the final. They were disappointed. The USA won once more, by 17–3. 'Playing unbeatable football under murky skies,' enthused the *New York Herald*, 'in a stormy atmosphere and before an excited and antagonistic crowd, the American rugby team raised the Stars and Stripes over Colombes Stadium yesterday afternoon. The Americans played better football than they had ever played before, using the French style of group playing to the bewilderment of their opponents and smashing through the French lines time after time with well-guarded individual plays which left the Frenchmen scattered the length of the field.'

Those two stunning victories by the rugby union players of a nation which had reputedly abandoned the game 40 years earlier gave rise to unseemly rumours in the French camp that the Americans had loaded their squad with American football stars. They had not. The bulk of them came from one US institution which had – apparently anachronistically – held true to the old code: Stanford University.

By the 1920s amateurism had worked its divisive way with rugby union in arguably the most dramatic fashion of any of the Victorian games. A slow-burning grievance burst into flame in the 1890s. The Rugby Union had since its inception resisted any form of payment to players. This plainly favoured those in happy receipt of a private income over those who had to work for a living. As more of the latter were apparently based in the north of England, and the bulk of the former in the south, the disagreement took on a regional flavour. In June 1893 the Yorkshire Rugby Union unanimously agreed to petition the full Rugby Union to allow players to be given 'broken time' payments, if playing rugby took them away from their regular jobs and consequently lost them a Saturday's pay. At the AGM of the Rugby Union in London that September, J.A. Miller of the Yorkshire RU proposed 'that players be allowed compensation for bona fide loss of time.'

Miller's motion was opposed by a southern amendment which condemned it as 'contrary to the true interest of the game'. Amid 'tremendous cheering' the amateurs won the vote by 282 to 136.

But the genie was loose. Two years later, in the July and August of 1895, 12 leading clubs left the Yorkshire Rugby Union and resolved at a meeting in Leeds 'to push forward as expeditiously as possible the formation of a Northern Rugby Football Union'. And on 29 August representatives of 21 Lancashire and Yorkshire rugby union clubs met at the George Hotel in Huddersfield to form the Northern Rugby Football Union. This union would allow broken-time compensatory payments.

Initially, that was the sum of their differences. They moved slowly towards permitting full professionalism (in July 1898) and establishing a league structure similar to association football (in 1907). But the founding fathers of rugby league football had not intended to create a game which would become so different from rugby union that when the two leading English sides from each code would finally meet in competition a century later in 1996 – when rugby union had liberated itself from its amateur strictures – Bath would prove to be as inept at league football as Wigan were lost in the union rules. They arrived gradually at the changes, driven partly by a spirit of independence and partly by a necessary desire to improve the appeal to spectators of a game which depended upon gate money. In 1897 the Northern Union abolished the line-out and altered the scoring system, improving the reward for a try. In 1906 the Northern Union reduced the number of players in a team from 15 to 13. And in 1922 the Northern Rugby Football Union decided that its name was too parochial, and became the Rugby Football League.

They were motivated in this change by the fact that their code was, in 1922, played in two other countries – Australia and New Zealand. This, for a modest organisation which had initially restricted its own membership to clubs based between the north bank of the River

Trent and the Scottish border, seemed dizzily expansionist. The breakaway rugby players of the north of England had not intended to carry their game across the world. That was the function of rugby union, the game of the public schools and of the universities, and consequently of the district commissioners and army subalterns – of those who believed, in the words of the public school headmaster Hely Hutchinson Almond, that rugby football 'is the best instrument which we possess for the development of manly character'. The early proselytisers of rugby league were certainly interested in manly character, but were more concerned with the survival of their isolated professional sport than in the dissemination around the world of muscular Christianity.

Rugby league, as a result, seeped slowly overseas. It arrived in New Zealand in the early years of the twentieth century, and in 1907 A.H. Baskerville organised a New Zealand Rugby League team to tour England. The All Blacks travelled via Australia, where in August they discovered a situation of seething discontent. Alec Burdon, one of the most respected Australian rugby union players of his day, had broken his shoulder in a state match. The injured Burdon had received so little consideration from the New South Wales Rugby Union that several of his fellows were attracted by the new code. The travelling All Blacks were therefore invited to play three exhibition matches against a scratch squad of Sydney footballers. After those games the New Zealanders travelled on to England, where in the January and February of 1908 they played the first rubber of three international rugby league Test matches against England, and won the series 2–1. Back in Sydney the New South Wales Rugby Football League was hurriedly established on 8 August 1907; by April of the following year nine Australian teams were competing in a league; and by 18 November 1908 an Australian rugby league side was beating England at Everton Football Club's ground in Liverpool before 7,000 spectators.

The game travelled not much further. Throughout the twentieth – century rugby league served as an alternative to those rugby union players who required financial compensation or wages, and the game consequently put down roots in most of the rugby-playing countries. There were occasional attempts to evangelise the sport. In November 1954 Australia and New Zealand played two 'propaganda matches' in California. The first match was abandoned in dense fog after six minutes; at the second, 4,554 people saw Australia win by 30–13. The Los Angeles sponsors lost almost £2,000; the English Rugby

League Council dropped £800; and the Australian and New Zealand authorities spent £450. Rugby league failed to translate to the United States of America, a country which had already its own professional offshoot of the handling football game.

Even in those countries of the old Empire which adhered to rugby, the professional attractions of league were lessened by an easy-going attitude on the part of the unionists to the principles of amateurism. Nobody took the disciplines of no payment as seriously as did the British, and many other countries did not take them seriously at all. While English and Scottish rugby union players were, well into the twentieth century, being expelled from the game for the crime of writing a book, New Zealanders, Frenchmen and – it was be loudly whispered – even the occasional Welshman could find themselves housed, fed and watered by their amateur clubs. Rugby union was the establishment's game: it had the schoolboys, the media coverage and the blessing of the state. Rugby league, which had only ever come into existence as the result of union's perverse refusal to compensate its lower-class players for their loss of earnings, would never have been able to compete with the parent game on a level playing field. Few countries other than England and Scotland suffered this terrible disruption; none of them suffered it to the same extent; and the overweening supremacy of rugby union players from the Southern Hemisphere would stand at the end of the century as a bleak memorial to the debilitating legacy of abandoned amateurism.

The dispute between professionalism and amateurism was not only concerned with the payment of athletes and its corrosive effect on their spiritual well-being. It was also a running debate on the role of spectators. Many missionaries of amateurism believed that spectator sports corrupted not only the paid performer, but also the paying customer – that hysterical, chain-smoking youth whom Baron Baden-Powell had observed hanging over the advertising hoardings. It would have been inconceivable to such men that, before the twentieth century was done, intelligent, cultured and sensitive people would be able to watch the half-brother of rugby football and describe what they had seen as art.

Art form or not, association football has been Great Britain's most notable contribution to international sport and to the global entertainment industry. It differed from the high imperial games chiefly in that soccer was rarely the chosen sport of the governing classes: it travelled not with the diplomatic corps, but in the kit-bags and holdalls of private soldiers, or merchants, railway workers, miners and schoolteachers. Soccer was given no entrée. It was rarely delivered, along with Christianity, lighthouses, and a British legal system, to colonised countries; which is why soccer – the most successful of the empire games – thrived better in most countries of the world other than the old dominions, where it was historically overshadowed by rugby and cricket, or by squash, or badminton, or tennis. Soccer was loved and accepted not because of its associations with the power and mystique of the British Empire, but for itself.

In Australia, for instance, association football, which was introduced to New South Wales in the 1880s, was a century later no more than the fifth most popular spectator team sport in the country, and attracted fewer participants than ten other physical recreations. The game fared no better in New Zealand, was hardly enjoyed at all by the whites of South Africa, lagged a long way behind cricket in the West Indies, was barely played in India and Pakistan, attracted negligible support in Canada, and mystified most of the population of the United States of America. In almost every other nation of the world – the nations which had not been taught a bewildering variety of other British sports along with the English language – it had become by the second half of the twentieth century incomparably the biggest and most popular game for spectators and participants alike.

Nobody saw it coming. 'Football will not catch on here,' wrote the celebrated Brazilian author Graciliano Ramos in 1921. 'It is like borrowed clothes that do not fit. For a foreign custom to establish itself in another country it must be in harmony with the people's way of life, and we already have the corn straw ball game . . .'

Twenty-seven years before Ramos's spectacularly misplaced prediction, in the spring of 1894 a young man had disembarked at the port of Santos with two round leather balls and a set of association football rules in his cabin trunk. Charles Miller had been born in Brazil, but he was sent home to be educated in Hampshire, where he fell for the game of soccer. When he returned to work with the Sao Paulo Railway Company, Miller persuaded the Sao Paulo Athletic Club, a body of expatriates chiefly devoted to cricket, to take up the sport. A tournament was organised, mainly between the young British men who worked for the railway, the gas company and the London Bank, all of which were British-owned. In the first 20 years of the next century, state championships were formed throughout Brazil, and in the September of 1914 a Brazilian national squad played its first match, losing 0–3 to Argentina.

Miller's story had either been anticipated or would be repeated throughout Europe and South America. As early as May 1865 British residents in Argentina had started the Buenos Aires Football Club. Newell's Old Boys followed, as did River (not Rio) Plate and 1903 Racing Club. Boca Juniors was founded by an Irishman. In 1891 Alexander Hutton, the director of the English High School, formed the Argentine Association Football League. On 16 May 1901 the Argentine national side played the first international soccer matches to take place anywhere outside Great Britain, when they defeated Uruguay 3–2 in Montevideo. Four years later, in 1905, those representative matches were given extra significance by the donation of a trophy from the English grocer (and South American tea magnate) Sir Thomas Lipton: the unsuccessful international yachtsman of an earlier chapter.

For 20 years on each side of the turn of the century, nobody could escape the game, and it seemed that nobody wanted to. Soccer insinuated itself irresistibly into the body of nations. The first game was played in Turkey in 1895, when a group of British expatriates and Greek students competed in Smyrna. Teams such as Galatasary and Fenerbahce were founded ten years later. The governors of the crumbling Ottoman Empire were suspicious of this western implant, however (not least because it apparently originated with Englishmen and Greeks), and when in 1900 a group of young Turks met at a house to translate a copy of the game's English rules into Turkish:

> . . . a palace spy heard of the meeting, entered the building with a detachment of soldiers and arrested the conspirators.
>
> His worst suspicions were confirmed when he discovered a pump, corner-post flags, and multi-coloured shirts. In his report the shirts were described as uniforms, and the rules which the unlucky enthusiasts were translating as 'proclamations'. The football itself, which further search revealed, was called a 'top', which in Turkish means a cannonball. The offenders were banished . . .

International football was a child as much of the British industrial revolution as of the British Empire. For 60 years after the game's seminal formulation in 1863, British traders and workmen were to be found in every friendly country of the world, and in several hostile ones. The Austrian Willy Meisl left behind a classical account of the pervasive British cultural influence on independent central European states. 'In the old Austrian monarchy, soccer started almost simultaneously in Prague, Vienna and Graz, the capital of Styria,' wrote Meisl in 1955 of that lost nineteenth-century world.

> Vienna possessed a sizeable British colony. A number of British firms had branches or representatives in Austria's metropolis. An English gasworks had the licence to light the capital: English artists appeared on the stage; English typewriters, caps, clothes, shoes, anything and everything English was in demand. Gandon of the said gasworks; Lowe, manager of a hat manufacturers; Blyth of the haberdashers and gentleman's fashion house, Stone and Blyth; Shires, who represented Underwood [the typewriter company]; Blackey, manager of the engineering firm, Clayton and Shuttleworth; the Rev. Hechler of Vienna's Anglican Church – these were some of the men who founded the first two football clubs in Vienna.

The British influence is manifested in the names of the two oldest organisations, the first Vienna FC and the Vienna Cricket and Football Club (from which, via the Wiener Amateur SV, the present FK Austria descended). Although very few of its members and hardly any of its supporters had ever seen, let alone played cricket, the latter team was known only as the 'Cricketers', whilst the other has remained the 'Vienna' to this day.

Just as AC Milan began its life in 1899 as Milan Cricket and Football Club, and to this day rejects the Italian spelling of the city of Milano in deference to its British origins. Just as the title of the first Spanish football club, the Athletic Club of Bilbao, would retain the name given to it by its founding British seamen and miners back in 1898. Just as the oldest Soviet club Dynamo Moscow would continue to play in the blue and white colours of Blackburn Rovers, which had been given to them by their Lancastrian founders, Harry and Clement Charnock of the Orekhovo cotton mill, in 1887. And just as the most successful club in Accra, the capital of Ghana, would be known throughout the second half of the twentieth century as Hearts of Oak . . .

The Football Association allowed its game to become a professional sport in 1885 (the Scottish FA followed in 1893), and British soccer thus avoided the messy divorce which would damage rugby throughout the twentieth century. But professionalism was allowed in large part to permit the amateur administrators to retain their hold on the game. The hearts of those men were captured by the pretensions of amateurism. N.L. Jackson, the assistant secretary of the FA in the early 1880s, founded the epitome of footballing amateurism, the Corinthians AFC.

Corinthians, who would only draw their players from public school or Oxbridge men, made it a rule never to enter League or Cup competitions, and yet for 20 years after their foundation in 1882 they considered themselves to have a claim of right on the English international side (which was frequently beaten by its only early rival, Scotland). Some of the Corinthians' virtues, such as their adoption of the passing game, and their early tours to such places as South Africa, could later be seen as positively beneficial. Some of their habits, such as the one of ignoring the penalty kick law after its introduction in 1891 (Corinthians believed that no gentleman could knowingly commit a penalty offence, and so if one was awarded against them their goalkeeper would walk away from his goals; and if one was awarded to them they would deliberately kick it wide), were simply charming.

But we can hear the echo of Corinthian voices in many of the errors which dogged British football during the first half of the twentieth century. When the International Football Federation (FIFA) was formed in France in 1904, no British association would join in at first. They relented in 1906, but then withdrew in 1920 following a dispute over how soon the footballers of the defeated First World War nations – Germany, Austria and Hungary – should be allowed back into international competition. They rejoined in 1924, but quickly pulled out again because FIFA believed that amateur footballers – the ones who were allowed into the Olympics – should be paid broken-time payments, and the British authorities did not. Britain was right, claimed the Welsh, Scottish and English FAs, because most of the rest of FIFA consisted of younger bodies 'and in consequence cannot have the knowledge which only experience can bring'.

The English FA was quickly to gain even more experience of amateurism. In 1927 it was informed by anonymous letter that Crook Town, an amateur club in the Northern League, was paying broken-time money to its players. Following investigations the FA banned every Crook player and official indefinitely from football, expelled Crook Town from the Northern League (which they led), and expunged the club's name from their records.

Crook's former secretary retaliated by sending the FA a dossier which fingered 20 other northern clubs for committing the same offence. By the time the FA had finished scouring the Augean stables of Durham football two years later, they had banned no fewer than 1,000 officials and 341 players, fined nine clubs, effectively wiped out the bedrock of soccer in County Durham (Bishop Auckland AFC alone lost 46 players and almost its whole administration) and had been accused for their efforts of being 'little Mussolinis' with no concern for working-class football in the north of England.

A few months after the cut-and-burn conclusion of the Durham affair Sir Frederick Wall, who was the (amateur) secretary of the Football Association between 1895 and 1934, received a letter from Uruguay inviting the English national team to take part in an inaugural World Cup competition in 1930.

Wall wrote back on 30 November 1929. 'Dear Sir,' he said, 'the letter of the 10th ultimo from the Associacion Uruguaya De Football inviting a Representative Team of the Football Association to visit Uruguay in July and August next to play in the Worlds championship in Montevideo has been considered by our International Committee.

'I am instructed to express regret at our inability to accept the invitation.'

They were unmistakable tones: the accent of the men who had developed sport and given it to the twentieth century, and who now wished only to retreat inside their carapace. For they were shy boys at heart, and had not intended to rule the world . . .

Bibliography

Bird, Dennis L., *Our Skating Heritage* (London, 1979)

Birley, Derek, *Land of Sport and Glory: Sport and British Society, 1887–1910* (Manchester, 1995)

Blunden, Edmund, *Cricket Country* (London, 1945)

Brown, Nigel, *Ice Skating: A History* (London, 1959)

Bryson, Bill, *Made in America* (London, 1994)

Burnett, John, *Sporting Scotland* (Edinburgh, 1995)

Carey, John (ed.), *The Faber Book of Reportage* (London, 1987)

Cashman, Richard, *Patrons, Players and the Crowd: The Phenomenon of Indian Cricket* (New Delhi, 1980)

Cock, O.J., *A Short History of Canoeing in Britain* (London, 1974)

Dickens, Charles, *The Pickwick Papers* (London, 1837)

Everton, Clive, *The Embassy Book of World Snooker* (London, 1993)

The Football Association's Book for Boys (London, 1961)

Fraser, George MacDonald, *Flashman at the Charge* (London, 1973)

Geddes, Olive, *A Swing Through Time* (Edinburgh, 1992)

George, Dorothy M., *London Life in the Eighteenth Century* (London, 1925)

Golesworthy, Maurice, *The Encyclopaedia of Association Football* (London, 1957)

Gorn, Elliott J. and Goldstein, Warren, *A Brief History of American Sports* (New York, 1993)

Green, Benny, *A History of Cricket* (London, 1988)

Gurney, Gerald, *Table Tennis: The Early Years* (London, 1994)

Hamilton, Ian (ed.), *The Faber Book of Soccer* (London, 1992)

Harvey, Charles (ed.), *Sport International* (London, 1960)

Holt, Richard, *Sport and the British: A Modern History* (Oxford, 1989)

Homer (trans. E.V. Rieu), *The Odyssey* (London, 1946)

Hopkirk, Peter, *The Great Game: On Secret Service in High Asia* (Oxford, 1990)

Hutchinson, Roger, *Camanachd: The Story of Shinty* (Edinburgh, 1989)

James, C.L.R., *Beyond a Boundary* (London, 1963)

Jeffery, Gordon, *European International Football* (London, 1965)

Judd, Denis, *Empire: The British Imperial Experience from 1765 to the Present* (London, 1996)

Lewis, Tony, *Double Century: The Story of MCC and Cricket* (London, 1987)

Lowerson, John, *Sport and the English Middle Classes, 1870–1914* (Manchester, 1993)

McIlvanney, Hugh, *McIlvanney on Football* (Edinburgh, 1994)

MacLennan, Hugh Dan, *Shinty: Celebrating Scotland's Game* (Nairn, 1993)

Mandell, Richard D., *Sport: A Cultural History* (New York, 1984)

Mangan, J.A. (ed.), *The Cultural Bond: Sport, Empire, Society* (London, 1992)

Marquesee, Mike, *Anyone but England: Cricket and the National Malaise* (London, 1994)

Mason, Tony (ed.), *Sport in Britain: A Social History* (Cambridge, 1989)

Miroy, Nevil, *The History of Hockey* (London, 1986)

Morris, James, *Pax Britannica: The Climax of an Empire* (London, 1968)

Morris, James, *Heaven's Command: An Imperial Progress* (London, 1975)

Morris, James, *Farewell the Trumpets: An Imperial Retreat* (London, 1978)

Morris, Jan, *The Matter of Wales* (Oxford, 1984)

Morris, Jan, *Hong Kong, Xianggang* (London, 1988)

Moyes, A.G., *The Changing Face of Cricket* (London, 1966)

O Maolfabhail, Art, *Caman: 2,000 Years of Hurling in Ireland* (Dundalk, 1973)

Oliver, Guy, *The Guinness Record of World Soccer* (London, 1992)

Pakenham, Thomas, *The Scramble for Africa* (London, 1991)

Pearson, Harry, *The Far Corner: A Mazy Dribble Through North-East Football* (London, 1994)

Plumb, J.H., *England in the Eighteenth Century* (London, 1950)

Pottle, Frederick A. (ed.), *Boswell's London Journal, 1762–1763* (Yale, 1950)

Prebble, John, *The Lion in the North: One Thousand Years of Scotland's History* (London, 1971)

Rea, Chris, *Rugby: A History of Rugby Union Football* (London, 1977)

Rea, Frederick (ed. Campbell, John Lorne), *A School in South Uist: Reminiscences of a Hebridean Schoolmaster, 1890–1913* (London, 1964)

Ritchie, Andrew, *King of the Road: An Illustrated History of Cycling* (London, 1975)

Robertson, Max, *The Encyclopaedia of Tennis* (London, 1974)

Robertson, Max, *Wimbledon 1877–1977* (London, 1977)

Rous, Stanley, *Football Worlds: A Lifetime in Sport* (London, 1978)

Seymour, Harold, *Baseball, The Early Years* (New York, 1960)

Smith, David B., *Curling: An Illustrated History* (London, 1981)

Somerville, E.O.E. and Ross, Martin, *The Irish R.M. Complete* (London, 1928)

Taylor, James, *Curling: The Ancient Scottish Game* (Edinburgh, 1884)

Topolski, Daniel, *True Blue: The Oxford Boat Race Mutiny* (London, 1989)

Turner, Michael R. (ed.), *Parlour Poetry* (London, 1967)

Vamplew, Wray, and others (eds.), *The Oxford Companion to Australian Sport* (Oxford, 1992)

Vincent, Ted, *Mudville's Revenge: The Rise and Fall of American Sport* (Nebraska, 1981)

Wallace, Carlton, *The Boy's Book of Sport* (London, 1951)

Walvin James, *The People's Game: The History of Football Revisited* (Edinburgh, 1994)

Whitcher, Alec E., *An Intimate Talk on Soccer, the Ace of Games* (Brighton, 1944)

Whitton, Kenneth, and Jamieson, David A., *Fifty Years of Athletics, 1883–1933* (Edinburgh, 1933)

Wood, Revd J.G., *The Boy's Modern Playmate: A Book of Games, Sports and Diversions* (London, 1868)

Index